The War on
ISIS

Hal Marcovitz

ReferencePoint
Press®

San Diego, CA

Hillside Public Library

© 2019 ReferencePoint Press, Inc.
Printed in the United States

For more information, contact:
ReferencePoint Press, Inc.
PO Box 27779
San Diego, CA 92198
www.ReferencePointPress.com

ALL RIGHTS RESERVED.
No part of this work covered by the copyright hereon may be reproduced or used in any form or by any means—graphic, electronic, or mechanical, including photocopying, recording, taping, web distribution, or information storage retrieval systems—without the written permission of the publisher.

LIBRARY OF CONGRESS CATALOGING-IN-PUBLICATION DATA

Names: Marcovitz, Hal, author.
Title: The War on ISIS/by Hal Marcovitz.
Description: San Diego, CA: ReferencePoint, Inc., 2019. | Includes
  bibliographical references and index. | Audience: Grades 9–12.
Identifiers: LCCN 2018005891 (print) | LCCN 2018007712 (ebook) | ISBN
  9781682824788 (eBook) | ISBN 9781682824771 | ISBN 9781682824771¬ (hardback)
Subjects: LCSH: IS (Organization) | Terrorism—Middle East. |
  Terrorism—Religious aspects—Islam. | Middle East—History—21st century.
Classification: LCC HV6433.I722 (ebook) | LCC HV6433.I722 M317 2019 (print) |
  DDC 363.3250956—dc23
LC record available at https://lccn.loc.gov/2018005891

CONTENTS

IMPORTANT EVENTS IN THE WAR ON ISIS

2003
The United States and its allies invade Iraq to oust dictator Saddam Hussein, who is believed to have obtained weapons of mass destruction. The invasion touches off warfare between Shiite and Sunni Muslims in Iraq.

2010
US air strikes kill two leaders of the Islamic State of Iraq: Abu Ayyub al-Masri and Abu Omar al-Baghdadi. Abu Bakr al-Baghdadi takes command of the group.

1971
Abu Bakr al-Baghdadi, who will rise to command ISIS, is born in Samarra, Iraq.

2004
Abu Bakr al-Baghdadi is arrested as a suspected Sunni terrorist by the US military and is imprisoned for ten months in a US Army detention facility.

1970 / 2002   2004   2006   2008   2010

2001
Airliners hijacked by Islamist terrorists slam into the World Trade Center in New York City; the Pentagon in Washington, DC; and a field in Shanksville, Pennsylvania, killing nearly three thousand Americans and sparking the US invasion of Afghanistan.

2008
More than seventeen thousand members of al Qaeda in Iraq are believed to have been either killed or imprisoned by US forces; survivors flee into the Iraqi desert and form a new group: the Islamic State of Iraq.

2006
Abu Musab al-Zarqawi, the leader of the Sunni militant group al Qaeda in Iraq, is killed in a US air strike.

2007
The United States begins troop withdrawals from Iraq.

2011
The Arab Spring rebellions against dictators are staged in Libya, Tunisia, Egypt, and Syria; jihadists from the Islamic State in Iraq slip into Syria to form the al-Nusra Front.

2014
In January, ISIS invades Syria and takes the city of Raqqa; in June, ISIS overpowers the Iraqi army and takes the city of Mosul; in September, forty nations, including the United States, form the Global Coalition to Defeat ISIS and begin an offensive against the jihadist group.

2013
Abu Bakr al-Baghdadi announces that he has merged the Islamic State in Iraq with the al-Nusra Front, naming the new group the Islamic State in Iraq and Syria, or ISIS.

2016
Global Coalition forces retake the Iraqi cities of Hit, Rutbah, and Fallujah; by the fall, they prepare to retake Raqqa and Mosul.

| 2011 | 2012 | 2013 | 2014 | 2015 | 2016 |

2012
The US Defense Intelligence Agency issues a report warning President Barack Obama of the likelihood of a jihadist movement capable of taking over territory in Iraq and Syria; concerned that the US military would be drawn into another long war in the Middle East, Obama takes no action.

2017
ISIS is ousted from Raqqa and Mosul; in December, government officials in Iraq and Syria declare victory over ISIS.

2015
The Global Coalition wins its first significant victory when it defeats ISIS in the Syrian city of Kobani.

ISIS: A Threat to Global Security

On the night of July 13, 2013, the sounds of bombs and gunfire suddenly rocked two neighborhoods in the city of Baghdad in Iraq. As police officers rushed to the scenes of the explosions, many of them were cut down by gunfire. Hours later, the group responsible for the attacks, the Islamic State in Iraq and Syria, or ISIS, claimed it had killed more than 120 people.

The attacks were staged outside the walls of two prisons in Baghdad, which held hundreds of militants who had been imprisoned over the years for violent attacks against the people of Iraq. ISIS fighters used bombs and mortar shells to blow holes in the prison walls while cutting down police officers and prison guards with gunfire. In all, some five hundred militants were freed in the attacks, which ISIS labeled its Breaking the Walls campaign. "It's not easy to quickly hide five hundred prisoners in an area controlled by an enemy army, but [ISIS] had planned their escape well," says journalist Benjamin Hall. "As continued attacks around Baghdad diverted forces, the prisoners escaped by foot, fleeing in all directions from the prison. They headed to various meeting points in the surrounding countryside, where convoys of cars were waiting to ferry them away."[1]

The prison break was staged so that militants could be freed to join ISIS in its campaign of terrorism that it had been spreading across the Middle East since 2008, when the group formed in a remote desert region of Iraq. Throughout the remainder of 2013, ISIS staged similar attacks on other Iraqi prisons, freeing another one thousand militants so they, too, could join the ranks of the group.

Although ISIS committed incidents of terrorism on an almost daily basis, the carnage inflicted by the group was largely unknown outside the Middle East. That situation changed dramatically on August 19, 2014, when a video surfaced on the Internet showing a black-hooded ISIS soldier cutting the throat of James Foley, an American journalist whom the group had taken hostage. "You are no longer fighting an insurgency," the ISIS soldier declared. "We are an Islamic army."[2] Three weeks later ISIS released a new video showing the execution of a second American hostage, journalist Steven Sotloff.

To Murder and Enslave

Although the murders of Foley and Sotloff were shocking, by the early years of the 2000s Americans as well as others in the West had become all too familiar with Islamist terrorism. The attacks of September 11, 2001, took the lives of nearly three thousand Americans who were killed when terrorists hijacked airliners and crashed them into the World Trade Center in New York City, the Pentagon in Washington, DC, and a field in Shanksville, Pennsylvania. The Islamist terrorist group al Qaeda took responsibility for the attack.

By early 2018 the US State Department had identified no fewer than fifty separate organizations as Islamist terrorist groups. These groups vary in size, but their missions are strikingly similar: to bring down national governments and install in their places theocracies that would govern under the extreme edicts of fundamentalist Islamic law. In these theocracies, all people would live according to a literal interpretation of laws first written by Islamic scholars more than fourteen hundred years ago. To achieve this goal, their members are willing to resort to murdering and enslaving innocent civilians.

In the months following the Foley and Sotloff murders, no group on the State Department's list seemed more determined, or better able, to achieve its goal than ISIS. In 2016, Malcolm

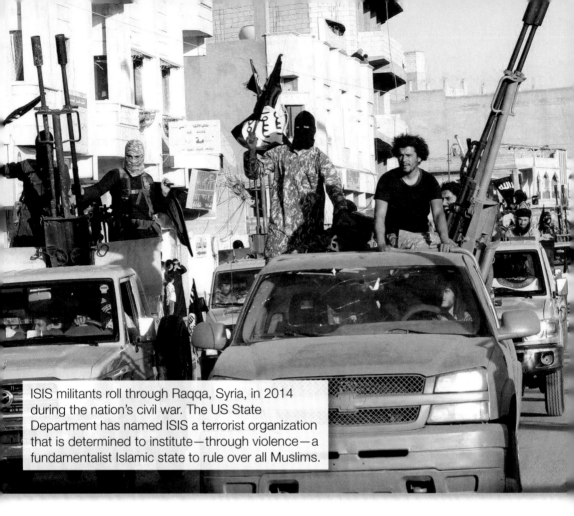

ISIS militants roll through Raqqa, Syria, in 2014 during the nation's civil war. The US State Department has named ISIS a terrorist organization that is determined to institute—through violence—a fundamentalist Islamic state to rule over all Muslims.

Nance, an American expert on counterterrorism, said, "The Islamic State in Iraq and Syria . . . has become the single most dangerous threat to global security since al-Qaeda. It is more than just a threat to America and the West, because it also poses an existential threat to Islam: its goal is to coopt and enslave 1.8 billion Muslims. . . . ISIS must be stopped at all costs."[3]

The Military Offensive Against ISIS

By the time of the Foley and Sotloff murders, ISIS had made it clear that it was interested in more than individual acts of terrorism. By the summer of 2014, ISIS soldiers laid siege to the Syrian city of Raqqa and the Iraqi city of Mosul. The Iraqi government appealed for military assistance; the United States responded by unleashing air strikes against ISIS. "[ISIS] poses a threat to the people of Iraq and Syria, and the broader Middle East— including American citizens, personnel and facilities," declared US president Barack Obama. "If left unchecked, these terrorists could pose a growing threat beyond that region, including to the United States."[4] In the United Kingdom, Foreign Secretary Philip Hammond said, "This is a poison, a cancer, what's going on in Iraq and Syria, and it risks spreading to other parts of the international community and affecting us all directly."[5]

> "The Islamic State of Iraq and Syria . . . has become the single most dangerous threat to global security since al-Qaeda."[3]
>
> —Malcolm Nance, an American expert on counterterrorism

The deaths of Foley and Sotloff were the final spark that led to the formation of the Global Coalition to Defeat ISIS. Dozens of nations joined the coalition. Its aim was to stage a military offensive against the Islamic State. The fighting on the ground was largely carried out by troops dispatched by the Iraqi and Syrian governments and by militias composed of Iraqi and Syrian ethnic groups. Coalition members launched numerous air strikes against ISIS that helped cripple the group, leading to its virtual defeat by late 2017.

Nevertheless, as the coalition made plans to strike against ISIS, other hostages suffered the same fates as Foley and Sotloff. Among them were American aid workers Peter Kassig and Kayla Mueller, British aid workers David Haines and Alan Henning, and Japanese journalist Kenji Goto. All of those victims are known to have been murdered by ISIS—their executions carried out in brutal fashion. Moreover, thousands of residents of Iraq and Syria were forced to endure the domination of ISIS—many were murdered, tortured, or enslaved. To world leaders, there was no question now that they faced a bloodthirsty group of terrorists steadfast in their resolve to kill innocent people in their quest to conquer the Middle East.

> "If left unchecked, these terrorists could pose a growing threat beyond that region, including to the United States."[5]
>
> —US president Barack Obama

CHAPTER ONE

The Rise of ISIS

The organization that evolved into ISIS emerged from two chaotic and catastrophic events that swept through the Middle East. The first event was the Iraq War, which commenced in 2003 when the United States and its allies invaded the Middle Eastern nation. The allies were convinced that Iraqi dictator Saddam Hussein had obtained weapons of mass destruction—such as nuclear missiles or bombs capable of spreading deadly radiation or biological agents—and intended to use them against his enemies. Although the invasion was brief—Saddam Hussein was ousted within a few months—the war caused a long-lasting, turbulent situation in Iraq. Revolution broke out on the streets of Iraqi cities as long-simmering hostilities among religious and ethnic groups surfaced. The fighting has continued into 2018.

The other spark that helped establish ISIS was the 2011 event known as the Arab Spring. Across the Middle East and North Africa, popular uprisings occurred in numerous Arabic countries ruled for decades by brutal dictators. Tunisia, Egypt, and Libya saw longtime despots ousted by revolutionaries who took to the streets. These revolutionaries were often assisted by military leaders who turned against their commanders. The Arab Spring also reached Syria, but Syrian president Bashar al-Assad proved to be far more resilient than other Arab leaders. He remained in power as his country plummeted into a long and bloody civil war. That conflict led to chaos and lawlessness throughout Syria. This provided prime turf for a renegade regime to establish itself, knowing that the government lacked both the will and resources to mount a military challenge against it.

One group that formed during these tumultuous times was al Qaeda in Iraq, founded by the Jordanian-born militant Abu Musab al-Zarqawi. His group maintained an alliance with the remnants of the original al Qaeda organization, which planned and executed the September 2001 terrorist attacks in the United States. Al Qaeda in Iraq was composed of members of the Islamic sect known as Sunnis, who saw as their mission the ouster of the American military that was attempting to bring order to the chaos that erupted after the defeat of Saddam Hussein. But Abu Musab al-Zarqawi also sought to eliminate the Iraqi leaders who came to power after Saddam Hussein's ouster. These Muslims were members of a sect of Islam known as Shia; its followers are known as Shiites. "Zarqawi's hatred of Shi'a was all consuming," says William McCants, a former adviser to the US State Department on Islamist extremist groups. "To his mind, the Shi'a were not just fifth columnists, selling out the Sunnis to the Americans. They were servants

During the Arab Spring of 2011, the people of several Arab nations rose up against the oppressive regimes that ruled them. Here, Egyptian protesters clash with the police forces of Hosni Mubarak, who had held power for thirty years.

of the Antichrist, who will appear at the end of time to fight against the Muslims. The Americans served the same master."[6]

The First Caliphs

To understand the meaning and ramifications of these events, one needs to look back to the founding of the Islamic faith more than fourteen hundred years ago. Islam was founded in 610 CE by Muhammad, a prophet who hoped to unite the Arab peoples by preaching the existence of one god, Allah. The name for the religion founded by Muhammad—Islam—is derived from the Arabic word *aslama*, which means "submitted." Therefore, a Muslim—or follower of Islam—is someone who submits himself or herself to the will of Allah. Over the next two decades, Muhammad's preachings and revelations were recorded in the Koran, which is the book of laws for the Islamic people.

When Muhammad died in 632, he was succeeded by one of his longtime followers, Abu Bakr. The elders of Islam named Abu Bakr the caliph, a word that derives from the Arabic *khalifa*, or "successor." (The realm ruled by the caliph is known as the caliphate.) Abu Bakr's reign as caliph began a period of instability for the faith. Abu Bakr died in 634, ending his reign after just two years. His successor, Umar ibn al-Khattab, was murdered by an assassin during the tenth year of his reign. The next caliph, Uthman ibn Affan, was also assassinated—his reign ending in 656.

> "Zarqawi's hatred of Shi'a was all consuming."[6]
>
> —William McCants, a former adviser to the US State Department

The fourth caliph—Muhammad's cousin Ali ibn Abi Talib—spent much of his reign putting down uprisings by rivals. Ali led his followers through many long, fierce, and bloody battles. During the fifth year of his reign, he was assassinated while praying in a mosque. He was succeeded by a rival, Muawiyah ibn Abi Sufyan. Many of Ali's followers refused to accept Muawiyah as caliph and broke away from his rule, forming a branch of Islam known as Shiat Ali, or the party of Ali. Today, that branch is known as Shia Islam. Those who

The Leader of ISIS: Abu Bakr al-Baghdadi

Abu Bakr al-Baghdadi, whose birth name is Ibrahim Awwad Ibrahim al-Badri, was born on July 1, 1971, into a farming family in Samarra, Iraq. Despite his family's agrarian background, Abu Bakr al-Baghdadi pursued studies of the Koran and eventually achieved a doctoral degree in 2007. He embraced an ultraconservative, literal interpretation of the Islamic holy book.

Following the US invasion of Iraq, Abu Bakr al-Baghdadi joined Sunni extremist groups seeking to expel the American military. He was arrested in 2004 for suspected extremist activism and spent ten months in Camp Bucca, a US Army detention facility. A former Bucca inmate who knew Abu Bakr al-Baghdadi later said, "Baghdadi was a quiet person. He had a charisma. You could feel that he was someone important. . . . But as time went on, every time there was a problem in the camp, he was at the center of it. He wanted to be the head of the prison—and when I look back now, he was using a policy of conquer and divide to get what he wanted, which was status. And it worked."

After Abu Bakr al-Baghdadi was released, he returned to his Islamic studies but remained active in the extremist movement, joining al Qaeda in Iraq. He rose in the group's ranks, becoming a close confidant of Abu Umar al-Baghdadi, who briefly served as head of the group following the death of Abu Musab al-Zarqawi. After Abu Umar al-Baghdadi's death, Abu Bakr ascended to leadership of ISIS.

Quoted in Terrorism Research & Analysis Consortium, "Islamic State of Iraq," 2017. www.trackingterrorism.org.

stayed loyal to Muawiyah became known as the Sunnis, from the Arabic word *sunna*, or "path." Sunni Islam has remained the dominant sect of Islam; an estimated 85 to 90 percent of the world's 1.8 billion Muslims follow the Sunni version of the faith.

Over the centuries, other faiths have gone through periods of upheaval that have often led to warfare. For example, during the sixteenth and seventeenth centuries the kingdoms of Europe endured long and bitter wars fought on religious grounds during the era known as the Protestant Reformation. During this era, the Protestant denominations of Christianity broke away from the dominion of the Catholic pope. Eventually, Catholics and Protestants bridged the differences that divided them and ended the blood-shed. But the hostility between many members of Shia and Sunni Islam has persisted—even after some fourteen hundred years. Well into the twenty-first century, violence between Shiites and Sunnis remains a common part of life in the Islamic world.

Waging Jihad

For two years the Sunni leaders of al Qaeda in Iraq waged a campaign of violence and mayhem, terrorizing innocent civilians as well as targeting members of the American military. Terrorist strikes, often carried out by suicide bombers, as well as kidnappings, assassinations, and attacks by snipers, were all daily occurrences in Iraq. But on June 7, 2006, the American military caught up with Abu Musab al-Zarqawi. Intelligence agents identified his hideout—a small house in the remote Iraqi village of Hibhib. Fighter jets were dispatched. A missile was fired from above, scoring a direct hit on the house. Minutes later American com-

In 2006 US forces killed Abu Musab al-Zarqawi, the al Qaeda leader who waged war against Shiite Muslims as well as US personnel in Iraq. Zarqawi's death was one of many successes in a US effort to eliminate the terrorist organization.

mandos arrived at the house, finding the al Qaeda leader barely alive. He died moments later.

The campaign to wipe out al Qaeda in Iraq did not end with the death of Abu Musab al-Zarqawi. American commandos relentlessly staged missions to eliminate the organization. Members of the terrorist group were rounded up and imprisoned during a door-to-door search in Iraqi cities or were killed in firefights or aerial attacks.

The US military's campaign all but wiped out al Qaeda. By 2008 an estimated twenty-four hundred members of the group had been killed, and another fifteen thousand were imprisoned. The remaining members of the group fled into the northern Iraqi desert, hiding in remote villages.

> "O soldiers of the Islamic State . . . erupt volcanoes of jihad everywhere. Light the earth with fire against all dictators."[7]
>
> —ISIS leader Abu Bakr al-Baghdadi

But they regrouped in the desert under a new name: the Islamic State of Iraq. It was their belief that they had established an autonomous nation in the Iraqi desert—a caliphate that would wage jihad against the Americans and others who opposed them.

Jihad is an Arabic term that means "holy struggle." Islamists regard jihad as their struggle to spread their faith. In the Koran, the term *jihad fi sabil illah* describes warfare against the enemies of Islam. Jihadists are, therefore, Islamist extremists willing to commit violence to protect and promote Islam.

The Islamic State in Iraq was first led by the militants Abu Ayyub al-Masri and Abu Omar al-Baghdadi, but both men were killed during a 2010 US air strike. The third in command, Abu Bakr al-Baghdadi, stepped forward as the new leader. (Abu Omar al-Baghdadi and Abu Bakr al-Baghdadi are not related—neither man was known by his birth name; in Arabic, the name *al-Baghdadi* means "one from Baghdad," the capital city of Iraq.) Abu Bakr al-Baghdadi would soon make his intentions clear, calling for Islamist militants to join him in the Iraqi desert. Writing on an Islamist website, he declared, "O soldiers of the Islamic State . . . erupt volcanoes of jihad everywhere. Light the earth with fire against all dictators."[7]

The Sons of Iraq

Still, by 2008 the ranks of the Islamic State remained sparse. "Where is this Islamic State of Iraq that you're talking about?" the wife of an Islamic State leader was reported to have asked. "We're living in a desert!"[8] Meanwhile, despite the ouster of Saddam Hussein and the killing of Abu Musab al-Zarqawi, the environment of Iraq remained turbulent and violent. Numerous groups—composed of both Shiite and Sunni extremists—waged war on one another. They also carried out attacks on the Iraqi government and American military, which had commenced a troop withdrawal in 2007 but, nevertheless, was still very much a presence in Iraq. The US military had, in fact, been assisted in its campaign against al Qaeda in Iraq by a coalition of Sunni tribal militias known as the Sons of Iraq. This group's leaders believed more in a unified Iraq than in a victory by Sunnis over Shiites. The militias were not affiliated with the Iraqi government or American military, but their members were armed and led by commanders who were willing to engage their enemies in battle. This episode in the Iraq War is known as the Sunni Awakening. It is regarded as a turning point in the conflict because it helped to quell the rise of jihadism in the country.

Despite the help provided by the Sons of Iraq, Iraqi president Nouri al-Maliki—a Shiite—remained suspicious of the group and ordered the militias disbanded in 2008. However, al-Maliki took no action to disband the many Shiite militias that remained in the country. Al-Maliki's crackdown on the Sunni militias proved to be a disastrous decision. The Iraqi army drove the Sunni fighters out of the cities, forcing many of them to flee into the desert, where they joined Abu Bakr al-Baghdadi and the Islamic State in Iraq. "Here in your midst has the market of Jihad opened and become easy to reach!" Abu Bakr al-Baghdadi declared on an Islamist website. "No mature, able-bodied person has any excuse to stay behind with those who refrain from making Jihad."[9]

Although estimates by intelligence agencies vary, by 2011 the ranks of the Islamic State in Iraq were believed to have included several hundred fighters. Many of them had been dis-

The Last Caliphate

During the era of the first caliphates—some fourteen centuries ago—the Arab world was far more advanced, cosmopolitan, and militarily stronger than the nations of the West. Indeed, at a time when London and Paris consisted of only a few thousand residents, Baghdad in Iraq and Cairo in Egypt each teemed with half a million citizens. "The caliphate administered huge areas with a standing army and a literate and [large] bureaucracy and Baghdad and Cairo were huge centres of trade and culture," says British historian Hugh Kennedy. "But it goes further than that. For some Muslims, the history of the caliphate points to a time when Muslims were God-fearing and devout, puritanical and self-disciplined and always willing to sacrifice their lives in the path of Allah." Historians believe this ancient past influenced ISIS in its quest for a new caliphate.

Over time, however, caliphates were also burdened with dissent, revolution, and forces beyond the control of their leaders. The last caliphate, which was established during the fourteenth century, evolved into the Ottoman Empire (based in what is now Turkey). The Ottoman rulers remained in power until just after World War I. The empire sided with Germany, Austria-Hungary, and the other Central powers during the conflict, ultimately suffering defeat when the war ended in 1918. Under the Treaty of Sèvres, signed in France in 1920, the Ottoman Empire was broken up into independent states, ending the empire and the last caliphate.

Hugh Kennedy, *Caliphate: The History of an Idea*. New York: Basic Books, 2016, p. xiv.

placed from their homes in Iraqi cities, but hundreds more from America and European countries were lured to Iraq by the Islamic State. The group appealed to them, largely through social media, to join the cause.

The Banner of the Islamic State

But Islamists much closer to Iraq than America or Europe were also flocking to join the Islamic State. The civil war in neighboring Syria, which had been sparked by the 2011 Arab Spring, had caused massive upheaval throughout the nation. To put down the uprising, Assad displayed no hesitancy in using the harshest measures against his own people. Assad is an Alawite, which is a sect of Islam closely related to Shia. Therefore, as an Alawite, Assad was regarded as an enemy by Abu Bakr al-Baghdadi and his Sunni followers.

Abu Bakr al-Baghdadi soon recognized that the Syrian president could recruit Syrian Sunnis displaced by Assad as al-Baghdadi pursued victory in the Syrian civil war. In 2011 he dispatched a deputy, Abu Muhammad al-Julani, to establish a rebel organization in Syria. Al-Julani slipped into Syria and met with Sunni Islamists who had been driven underground by the civil war. They formed the Jabhat al-Nusra—the Support Front for the People of Greater Syria, or, familiarly, the al-Nusra Front. "Syria would not have been ready for us if not for the Syrian revolution," al-Julani said later. "The revolution removed many obstacles and paved the way for us to enter the blessed land."[10]

Abu Bakr al-Baghdadi, the political and religious leader of ISIS, speaks at a mosque in Mosul, Iraq, in 2014. Al-Baghdadi spoke confidently of creating an Islamic caliphate in the region after portions of Iraq and Syria fell to ISIS militants.

The al-Nusra Front grew quickly, recruiting hundreds of Syrian Sunni extremists to its cause. On April 9, 2013, Abu Bakr al-Baghdadi posted an audio message on Islamist websites announcing a merging of groups. He stated, "We declare, keeping our trust in Allah, the abolishing of the name of the Islamic State of Iraq and the abolishing of the name of the al-Nusra Front, and joining them under one name—the Islamic State in Iraq and al-Sham—and also uniting the banner, which is the banner of the Islamic State."[11] In English, *al-Sham* is translated into the word *Levant*, which refers to the lands east of the Mediterranean Sea: Turkey, Syria, Lebanon, Jordan, and Israel. In English, the new organization was known as the Islamic State in Iraq and the Levant (ISIL). Another common name for the group is Daesh, which is an acronym based on the Arabic name for the Islamic State. However, it soon became most familiarly known in the West as the Islamic State in Iraq and Syria (ISIS).

> "Syria would not have been ready for us if not for the Syrian revolution. The revolution removed many obstacles and paved the way for us to enter the blessed land."[10]
>
> —Abu Muhammad al-Julani, the leader of the al-Nusra Front

The Fall of Mosul

Since its creation, ISIS has carried out many terrorist acts, but Abu Bakr al-Baghdadi made it clear the organization had a much wider purpose: to establish a traditional caliphate that would rule over the world's 1.8 billion Muslims. The caliphate would encompass the nations of the Middle East. The governments of those countries—whether they were democratically elected, ruled by royal families, or headed by vicious dictators—were to be ousted. The caliphate would adhere strictly to a literal interpretation of the Koran—enforcing a code of conduct known as sharia law. In Islam, sharia law is not a written set of laws, such as the US Constitution or the British Magna Carta. Rather, sharia law reflects the overall way of life of the Muslim people. There are different interpretations of sharia law, with some Muslims accepting more liberal forms of guidance while others, including leaders of ISIS, adhere to very strict and conservative versions. As head of ISIS, Abu Bakr al-Baghdadi planned to rule as caliph—the chief religious and political leader of the Islamic State. In July 2014, he discussed the establishment of the caliphate: "This is a duty upon the Muslims—a duty that has been lost for centuries. . . . The Muslims sin by losing it, and they must always seek to establish it."[12]

In late 2013 and early 2014, as civil war touched every corner of Syria, a fierce battle commenced for control of the Syrian city of Raqqa. On January 14, 2014, black-hooded militants claimed victory, raising a black flag adorned with Arabic lettering that read, "There is no god but Allah. Muhammad is the messenger of Allah." It was the flag of ISIS, and it would soon become a well-recognized symbol across the world. Raqqa represented the first major military victory for ISIS.

A more significant victory came six months later. On June 10, ISIS fighters swept through the northern Iraqi city of Mosul. They encountered little opposition from the Iraqi military. NBC News correspondent Richard Engel described the battle:

> When ISIS fighters arrived in Mosul, they were outnumbered by an enormous margin. Just hundreds of jihadists attacked two or three divisions of the Iraqi army, upward of twenty thousand men.
>
> The ISIS gunmen were willing to die for their cause, but the Iraqi soldiers decidedly were not. They cut and ran, leaving behind uniforms, weapons, and thousands of [vehicles]. . . . ISIS had tapped on the Iraqi army and found that it was as fragile as an egg. . . .
>
> Mosul was a game changer, the moment when ISIS surpassed al-Qaeda as the region's dominant jihadist group. . . . ISIS also wasn't content to embarrass the Iraqi army and take its weapons. It brutalized the soldiers it captured, lining up and executing seventeen hundred prisoners in a single incident. ISIS put the whole gory exercise online,

and some Sunnis secretly cheered. . . . ISIS, as radical as it was, was marching toward Baghdad promising to replant the Sunni flag. . . . The idea of the caliphate, even one stained in blood, also resonated with Sunni Muslims. It harked back to a time when the Islamic world, and Arabs in particular, were strong and leaders, instead of weak and divided as they have been for the last century. . . . Mosul was ISIS's breakout moment.[13]

Murderous Tactics

In the days following the capture of Mosul, ISIS fighters relentlessly pursued those whom they perceived as enemies. For example, when they entered Mosul's Badush prison, they rounded up and executed some six hundred Shiite inmates.

On July 5, 2014, Abu Bakr al-Baghdadi made a rare public appearance. Addressing worshippers in Mosul's Great Mosque of al-Nuri, he boldly declared himself caliph and demanded the obedience of the world's Muslims. He also warned his followers of the bloody conflict ahead: "Prepare your arms, and supply yourselves with piety. Persevere in reciting the Koran with comprehension of its meanings and practice of its teachings. This is my advice to you. If you hold onto it, you will conquer . . . and own the world."[14] When Abu Bakr al-Baghdadi made that speech, ISIS controlled some 34,000 square miles (88,060 sq. km) in Iraq and Syria.

Across the globe, political leaders were stunned by the sweeping success of ISIS. For months, ISIS waged a relentless campaign, easily overrunning cities in Iraq and Syria. The world had rarely seen a revolutionary movement mobilize so quickly and so successfully. And it had rarely seen a revolutionary movement resort to the murderous tactics that became the symbol of ISIS aggression.

CHAPTER TWO

Life Under ISIS

Farida Khalaf grew up in the northern Iraqi town of Kocho and hoped to become a math teacher. In the summer of 2014, however, ISIS soldiers swept through Kocho. Kalaf and many other residents there practice the Yazidi religion, which predates Islam. Soon after the arrival of ISIS in Kocho, Khalaf and many other Yazidi women and young girls were kidnapped—to be sold into slavery and raped by their masters. As for Yazidi men and boys, many—including Khalaf's father and brother—were murdered by ISIS. "I'd been traded like an animal in a livestock market," recalls Khalaf, who was sixteen years old at the time of her capture.

> The men who'd kidnapped and kept me captive had peddled me. They'd earned money by relinquishing me to other men who could now do with me as they pleased. Who regarded me as their "property," as their "slave." And all those involved behaved as if their dealings were perfectly legitimate and normal. How could these people justify their deeds before their God? Did they seriously believe, as they kept insisting, that He gave them the right to do this?[15]

Khalaf and the others were taken to Raqqa, where they were sold in a slave market. Khalaf spent about four months in ISIS captivity. In December 2014 Khalaf and seven other ISIS slaves—one only twelve years old—managed to slip away from their captors. Using a cell phone stolen from one of their captors, the escapees managed to contact family members who arranged to smuggle them out of ISIS territory and, eventually, to Germany.

Farida Khalaf was taken captive by ISIS in 2014 when her village in Iraq was occupied. Like many other female prisoners of ISIS, Khalaf suffered beatings and rapes and was eventually sold into slavery. Fortunately, she escaped her brutal masters.

After arriving in Germany, Khalaf enrolled in school. She hopes to eventually earn a college degree and realize her dream to teach math. "The fanatics who degraded us and treated us like objects are not going to stop me pursuing this goal," she insists. "I survived to prove to them that I'm stronger than they are."[16]

Sanctioning Slavery

ISIS believes it had the authority to murder the Yazidi men and boys and enslave the Yazidi women and girls because, in the eyes of the extremists, Yazidis are infidels: they do not follow

Islam and, therefore, are not deserving of rights. And since slavery, torture, lashings, beheadings, and other forms of punishment were common during the seventh century—when the Koran was written—ISIS believes such brutal behavior is sanctioned under Islamic law. Abu Muhammad al-Adnani, who was believed to be the second in command of ISIS before his death in 2016, once taunted the West with this comment: "We will conquer [you], break your crosses, and enslave your women. If we do not reach that time, then our children and grandchildren will reach it, and they will sell your sons as slaves at the slave market."[17]

Ehud Toledano, a professor at Tel Aviv University in Israel and an authority on slavery in the Islamist world, points out that the Prophet Muhammad tolerated slavery. ISIS leaders have embraced this fact as authority to enslave their enemies some fourteen hundred years later. "They are in full compliance with Koranic understanding in its early stages," says Toledano, "what the Prophet has permitted, Muslims cannot forbid."[18]

But many Islamic scholars insist that ISIS's interpretation of the Koran is wrong. They contend that Islam is a faith that preaches peace and recognizes the rights of non-Muslims. They believe ISIS leaders often take passages from the Koran or the hadith (a lengthy record of Muhammad's words and deeds) out of context as justification for committing horrific acts against innocent people. Salam al-Marayati, the executive director of the Los Angeles–based Muslim Public Affairs Council, says,

> Take, for example, how ISIS has been forcing ethnic Yazidi women into sexual slavery, a practice it says is rooted in historic precedence. Such a claim is absurd and false; yet the revelation has spurred a debate on sex slavery in Islam, as if the practice deserves any consideration at all, and as if ISIS deserves the kind of religious legitimacy conferred upon it by discussion of its proclamations.

The truth is that from a doctrinal, Islamic perspective, slavery is as an affront to the natural state of the freedom in which God created human beings that is tied to the first pillar of Islam (declaration of faith). All humans are equal before God and are distinguished only by their own good actions.[19]

The Hesba Division

Despite the debate over ISIS interpretations of the Koran, scholars agree that life in ISIS-controlled territories in many ways mirrored seventh-century society. Men were told they were not allowed to shave because ISIS believes shaving is immoral. Smoking tobacco and drinking alcoholic beverages were prohibited. Music could not be played outside one's home. The use of cell phones was banned. "If they found a cellphone in your pocket you would be killed,"[20] says Younis Abdullah, who was a resident of ISIS-occupied Mosul.

Muslim women were warned to dress conservatively when they left their homes. Moreover, they were not permitted to leave their homes unless accompanied by male relatives. And when women were outside their homes, they were under orders to cover their faces, arms, and hands. Women who were deemed to be dressing too provocatively were punished with public lashings. Some women were tortured with an instrument resembling a steel claw. In Mosul, the instrument was

> "If they found a cellphone in your pocket you would be killed."[20]
>
> —Younis Abdullah, who lived in ISIS-controlled Mosul

known as "the Biter" because ISIS used it to rip into the flesh of its victims. "The Biter has become a nightmare for us," said Fatima, a twenty-two-year-old Mosul woman who was able to escape from the city. "My sister was punished so harshly last month because she had forgotten her gloves and left them at home."[21]

Use of the Internet, a key recruiting tool, was strictly controlled and closely monitored in territories occupied by ISIS. Wisam, a

Attending ISIS Schools

ISIS policed schools in its occupied territory to ensure they were teaching curricula that conformed with the group's philosophy. Only boys were permitted to attend classes, and most of these focused on Islamic law and the lessons of the Koran—told from the ISIS perspective. But even classes that addressed such secular subjects as mathematics were heavily influenced by the ISIS worldview. For example, at the Kufa elementary school in Mosul, ISIS issued textbooks rife with its philosophy. According to a CBC News report, one math textbook contained the following problem: "There are 42 bullets and seven unbelievers in front of you. How many shots in your sniper rifle do you have for each?" An anti-ISIS activist in Raqqa known by the pseudonym Tim Ramadan described other ISIS teaching strategies. "In school, the books don't have math problems that ask you what two plus two is; the math problem is always two guns plus two guns equals what," Ramadan said. "They will bring a bomb to class to show it to the children and tell them they have nothing to fear from it because they are men, and the creative writing exercise is about a boy whose father carries out a suicide bombing."[']

Many parents withdrew their children from school and, instead, kept them home during the years of the ISIS occupation. One Mosul student whose parents would not let him attend school was thirteen-year-old Ahmad Firas. "We lost everything," Ahmad says. "Even our reading skills."

Quoted in Derek Stoffel, "Life Under ISIS: Mosul Residents Reflect on a Brutal Occupation," CBC News, March 22, 2017. www.cbc.ca.

Quoted in Fazel Hawramy, Shalaw Mohammed, and Kareem Shaheen, "Life Under Isis in Raqqa and Mosul: 'We're Living in a Giant Prison,'" *Guardian* (Manchester, UK), December 9, 2015. www.theguardian.com.

nineteen-year-old Mosul resident, quit his job as a photo editor at a local television station because it required him to use the Internet. He feared that ISIS would accuse him of using the Internet inappropriately—and that he would be punished. Instead, he found a job selling vegetables in a street bazaar. "I could not work online because the Internet is heavily monitored by ISIS,"[22] he says.

To enforce its laws, ISIS dispatched a police unit known as the Hesba Division. (In Arabic, *hesba* means "accountability.") Moreover, to make sure everyone followed the rules, the Hesba

Division erected video cameras throughout the ISIS-occupied cities so Hesba officers could spy on citizens. Large television screens were erected in public squares broadcasting ISIS rules and admonishing residents to follow them. Hesba Division officers patrolled constantly, often stopping civilians on the street and searching them for phones or other prohibited devices, such as laptops or tablet computers. And there was no easy method of escape: barriers were erected across streets that led out of the cities. Anybody attempting to leave was turned back.

Cruel Punishments

For the people of ISIS-occupied Syria and Iraq, getting caught with a cell phone or in violation of other rules would likely lead to cruel punishments. As many women knew, going out in public without one's face or hands properly covered could mean lashings. Consuming alcoholic beverages could also result in public lashings.

The death penalty was meted out for many offenses. Adultery, homosexuality, and apostasy—refusing to follow Islam as ISIS believed it should be followed—all carried the death penalty. Likewise, spying for a foreign power—which was broadly defined as taking up arms against ISIS—was also punishable by death.

Such harsh punishments were dispensed under ISIS's interpretation of the Islamic concept of *hudud*, an Arabic word meaning "limitations" or "restrictions." "The form of Hudud ISIS practices could be described as 'Hudud Ultra,'" says counterterrorism expert Malcolm Nance. "They have arranged for all punishments to be carried out in the precise manner of seventh-century Islam. In fact, ISIS has codified an excessive form of Hudud in order to eliminate any tolerance or compromise that was adopted since the Koran was written."[23]

> "[ISIS has] arranged for all punishments to be carried out in the precise manner of seventh-century Islam."[23]
>
> —Counterterrorism expert Malcolm Nance

Women in a shopping district in Raqqa, Syria, obey the rules for proper dress under strict Islamic law. While moving about in public women are expected to cover their bodies with traditional garments designed to protect their modesty.

Violators were often brought before an ISIS court that heard evidence and pronounced sentencing under the group's strict interpretation of sharia law. After their arrests, violators were typically held in ISIS prisons for many months, where they were beaten or otherwise tortured and fed little, bringing them to the brink of starvation. When, finally, they appeared before the ISIS court, their trials were brief and, invariably, concluded with the defendants learning their terrible fates. As Nance explains, "All actions in ISIS are religious and prophetic in nature and in which the punishment has to fit the Hudud. . . . They take the phrase 'eye for an eye' quite literally. If you have burned someone (or bombed them from the sky), you will be burned alive; if you have blown up a person with a rocket-propelled grenade, you will be killed with a rocket-propelled grenade."[24]

Other forms of the death penalty carried out by ISIS included decapitations, death by being buried alive, death by drowning, and death by falling—in other words, victims were thrown off the roofs of buildings. Death by falling was ISIS's preferred method of punishment for gay people.

Death by fire was often reserved for military prisoners. In 2015, months after the Global Coalition to Defeat ISIS had commenced air strikes against the Islamic State, a plane flown by Jordanian air force pilot Muath al-Kaseasbeh was shot down over Raqqa. ISIS executed al-Kaseasbeh by locking him in a cage, dousing him with gasoline, and setting him on fire. The episode was filmed by ISIS and aired on the Internet.

The Smugglers Who Saved the Yazidis

Many Yazidi women and girls were saved from slavery by an underground network of smugglers who helped spirit them out of ISIS captivity—sometimes by helping them slip past their guards and other times by delivering ransoms. "For [ISIS,] women and girls are nothing more than goods and our only option is to trade them like you would trade goods and products over the border," explained Abdullah Shrem, an Iraqi who traded in agricultural produce before the ISIS occupation. After ISIS took control, Shrem used his business skills to negotiate the release of some three hundred Yazidi women and girls.

The families of the captives often had to pay ransoms of tens of thousands of dollars. Sometimes the ransoms went directly to ISIS, but other times they went to the smugglers who helped the captives escape but still expected to be paid for their services. It was dangerous work; Shrem said he knew of more than twenty smugglers executed by ISIS for attempting to help the Yazidi captives.

Shrem put together his network of smugglers, drawing mostly from a pool of shadowy individuals who made their livings smuggling cigarettes into Iraq prior to the ISIS occupation. With tobacco use prohibited under ISIS, the smugglers found themselves out of work. Shrem found a way to make use of their skills. "No government or experts trained us," Shrem explained from his headquarters in a region of Iraq near the ISIS-controlled territory. "We learned by just doing it. . . . We gained the experience."

Quoted in BBC News, "Smugglers Help Enslaved Yazidis Escape Islamic State," August 18, 2015. www.bbc.com.

Quoted in Arwa Damon, Hamdi Alkhshali, and Bryony Jones, "Meet the Man Saving Yazidi Slaves from ISIS," CNN, June 2, 2016. www.cnn.com.

Oil Production Under ISIS

Foreign soldiers such as al-Kaseasbeh as well as the Yazidi were not the only people to suffer under ISIS. Other ethnic groups targeted by ISIS included about five hundred thousand Christians living in Iraq and Syria and about eighty thousand members of an ethnic group known as the Turkmens, most of whom lived in the Iraqi city of Tal Afar.

As for many others, despite the heavy hand wielded by ISIS, during the early months of the occupation the people living within the boundaries of the Islamic State were still able to go to their jobs and earn paychecks. Basic utilities, such as electricity and heating fuel, were still available. Food could be found in street markets. People living in the Islamic State were able to endure day-to-day life as long as they worshipped faithfully in their mosques and abided by ISIS's strict rules for personal behavior.

The ability of people living in the occupied territory to maintain an acceptable standard of living was due in no small part to the tremendous wealth acquired by ISIS soon after it conquered parts of Syria and Iraq. ISIS collected heavy taxes from the people living in the occupied territories; it also seized and looted banks in both countries. But most of ISIS's true wealth came from the oil fields it seized in Iraq and Syria, where it pumped as much as fifty thousand barrels a day out of the ground.

Even though ISIS was regarded as a rogue regime and was therefore banned from international energy markets, it still found customers for oil, which it exported from seaports it controlled in Iraq and Syria. ISIS's own public statements indicate that it had at times earned as much as $50 million a month selling oil.

The oil was sold through an underground network of smugglers for as little as ten dollars a barrel—about forty dollars per barrel less than crude oil was earning on world markets. Because its crude oil was so cheap, ISIS found many willing buyers in the underground oil market. The smugglers typically paid cash for the oil. The cash was then returned to the Islamic State by couriers.

Escaping ISIS

Thanks to the money earned through oil sales, ISIS was literally able to keep the lights on in its occupied territories. But starting in the fall of 2014, following the establishment of the Global Coalition to Defeat ISIS, the Islamic State was forced to spend virtually its entire treasury on defense. Most of ISIS's assets went to paying soldiers. By 2015 ISIS was estimated to have recruited some thirty thousand fighters, most of them foreigners who flocked to join the cause. Those soldiers had to be armed, which meant ISIS had to procure weapons and ammunition for them.

As ISIS diverted its assets to pay for the war against the Global Coalition, living conditions in the occupied territories of the Islamic State declined. Food was scarce. The delivery of public utilities—such as electricity and clean water—was often sporadic. The lack

The ground and air war against ISIS has reduced many Syrian and Iraqi cities to rubble. The displaced citizens of these regions have become refugees, flooding neighboring countries where they await a time when they can return home safely.

of electrical power or clean water was due largely to Global Coalition air strikes, which wiped out electricity-generating stations, power lines, and water-treatment plants. In fact, the inability of farmers to obtain water to irrigate their crops or electricity to run their farm machines helped lead to a food shortage. "Life is becoming more and more difficult," Maajid, a fifty-six-year-old Mosul mechanic and the father of eleven children, said in December 2015. "Even if you live in the worst part of the world, you need food, water and electricity to survive."[25]

> "Life is becoming more and more difficult. Even if you live in the worst part of the world, you need food, water and electricity to survive."[25]
>
> —Maajid, a fifty-six-year-old Mosul mechanic and the father of eleven children

As the war against ISIS intensified, living conditions for the people of Mosul, Raqqa, and the other cities in the Islamic State deteriorated further. Many people tried to escape but found the roadways out of the cities blocked by ISIS soldiers. They were turned back. Some refugees resorted to hiring smugglers who—for high fees—led them through the Iraqi and Syrian deserts to freedom. These journeys were often hazardous because ISIS buried land mines along many of the escape routes. In December 2015 Ali Mohammad, a police supervisor in the Iraqi town of Dibis, located just outside the ISIS-controlled territory, said, "Daesh has mined the path of people fleeing and my officers collected the bodies of five civilians who stepped on [land mines] last month."[26]

As the war against ISIS ramped up, the civilian death toll rose as well. Neighborhoods in Mosul, Raqqa, and other cities were reduced to rubble. Refugees from Syria and Iraq streamed into other countries. Some, like Farida Khalaf, were able to find cause for new hope. But many others driven from their homes remained in refugee camps—their homes and families destroyed in the war against the Islamic State.

CHAPTER THREE

The Path Toward War

Jejoen Bontinck had been raised a Catholic in the Belgian city of Antwerp, but in 2011—at the age of fifteen—he started dating a Muslim girl who insisted that if they continued to see one another, Bontinck would have to learn about Islam. He complied and eventually did more than study Islam—he converted to the faith.

Bontinck soon became a dedicated Muslim, praying five times a day at an Antwerp mosque. The mosque's imam, or religious leader, gave sermons emphasizing the peaceful nature of Islam and urged members to volunteer for charity work. But soon after Bontinck started attending the mosque, he was recruited by an Islamist group known as Sharia4Belgium, which maintained ties to armed jihadists in the Middle East. Leaders of Sharia4Belgium spent months radicalizing Bontinck—that is, indoctrinating him into a fundamentalist form of Islam based on a literal interpretation of the Koran.

In February 2013 Bontinck flew to Turkey to meet up with other young jihadists there. The group then made their way across the border into Syria and soon found themselves in an ISIS training camp, where they learned how to handle weapons and were schooled in the tactics of warfare.

Bontinck's recruitment and radicalization illustrates how ISIS searched for young fighters to swell its ranks in the months leading up to full-scale war. The group's fighters came not only from Middle Eastern states but from Western nations as well. And as ISIS drew thousands of young fighters to the Islamic State, leaders of Western nations grew increasingly concerned and ultimately came to the conclusion that a war against ISIS was inevitable.

Hillside Public Library

Recruiting Through Social Media

Just eleven days after beginning his training, Bontinck was arrested by ISIS fighters and tossed into a cell. His ISIS commanders had discovered that Bontinck had texted his family back home in Antwerp despite strict warnings by ISIS that new recruits were to have no contact with the outside world. Bontinck was then tortured; he was gagged and whipped with electrical cords over a four-day period. After six months Bontinck was released from his cell—after promising he would fight as an ISIS soldier. And, soon, Bontinck did see military action while participating in an ISIS attack near the Syrian city of Aleppo.

Jejoen Bontinck, a Belgian citizen, converted to Islam and was soon after recruited by a radical Islamic group online to fight in Syria. ISIS has successfully used social media to entice many Muslims worldwide to fight for its cause.

Bontinck's story is not unique. He is among some four thousand Europeans who made their way into Syria or Iraq to become ISIS soldiers. (About four hundred Americans are believed to have slipped into Syria and Iraq to join ISIS.) In Bontinck's case, he was recruited by a radical Islamist group that operated quite openly in Belgium and advocated for the creation of a European caliphate.

Although many similar groups were known to directly recruit members in Europe, ISIS also used social media to attract recruits from Europe and the United States. ISIS drew new recruits to Facebook pages, Twitter feeds, and other social media outlets that preached radical Islam and made bold promises to young people of a better life in the Islamic State. Jacob Siegel, a former US military intelligence officer, explains that

> "ISIS no longer depends on intermediaries to broadcast its barbarism. In this new environment, the group's media arm can upload its propaganda and see it spread globally in a matter of minutes or hours."[27]
>
> —Jacob Siegel, a former US military intelligence officer

starting in Iraq and later spreading to Syria after entering the war there in 2013, ISIS used social media to publicize its campaign of slaughter and threaten its enemies. The group's military prowess was enhanced by its reputation for brutality, spread by its own media efforts, which weakened its enemies' resistance and led some to flee from battle. On Twitter and in Facebook pages ISIS was making appeals as well as threats, attracting recruits and soliciting funding online. . . . ISIS no longer depends on intermediaries to broadcast its barbarism. In this new environment, the group's media arm can upload its propaganda and see it spread globally in a matter of minutes or hours.[27]

ISIS Threatens the West

ISIS's campaign to recruit young jihadists—either through organizations like Sharia4Belgium or through social media—posed a concern for officials in the West. They feared that the jihadists from Europe and America intended to travel to the Middle East, where they would be further radicalized, schooled in the techniques of terrorism, and then sent back to their home countries to kill innocent people. "What really worries American counterterrorism officials is that ISIS will prioritize launching attacks against the United States, will train Western recruits in bomb-making and send them back,"[28] Paul Cruickshank, a terrorism analyst at the Center for Law and Security at New York University, said in September 2014, as Western leaders started planning a military response to ISIS.

As for Bontinck, after participating in the battle near Aleppo, he decided he wanted nothing more to do with ISIS. Secretly, he contacted his family in Antwerp, telling them he wanted to come home. His father, Dimitri, traveled to Turkey and made contact with smugglers. For $300, the smugglers were able to find Bontinck in Syria and help him slip across the border.

After eight months in Syria—six months of which were spent in an ISIS prison—Bontinck was able to return to Belgium. But upon arriving home in Antwerp, he was arrested and charged with terrorism-related offenses. He eventually pleaded guilty and was sentenced to forty months in prison, but his sentence was suspended. Bontinck agreed to cooperate with prosecutors and testify against the leaders of Sharia4Belgium. His testimony helped Belgian authorities break up the group and imprison its leaders for lengthy jail sentences.

> "What really worries American counterterrorism officials is that ISIS will prioritize launching attacks against the United States, will train Western recruits in bomb-making and send them back."[28]
>
> —Paul Cruickshank, a terrorism analyst at the Center for Law and Security at New York University

The Heavy Toll of War

The recruitment of young would-be jihadists like Bontinck concerned officials in America and Europe, but for leaders of Middle Eastern countries, they represented a very real threat. With ISIS's

Europeans United Against ISIS

Forty European nations, including many countries that had seldom faced the threat of terrorism, joined the fight against ISIS. Among them were Denmark, Iceland, Finland, Norway, the Netherlands, and Luxembourg. These and other European countries joined the Global Coalition to Defeat ISIS and contributed to the effort to defeat the Islamic State.

Denmark, for example, found itself with cause for concern when a Danish-born jihadist told a newspaper in August 2014 that he would expect ISIS to target Denmark for a terrorist attack. "We have become very international and Denmark is high up on the list, believe me," the jihadist, who identified himself as ÖA, told the newspaper. "It is an open war now. ISIS has said that all infidels should be battled. They should be eliminated and soon it will be Denmark's turn."

A short time later, Danish lawmakers approved the country's membership in the Global Coalition. Danish prime minister Helle Thorning-Schmidt subsequently ordered her country's military to dispatch six fighter jets for service in the Middle East. "No one should be ducking in this case," Thorning-Schmidt said. "Everyone should contribute."

Quoted in *Local*, "Denmark 'High on ISIS's List': Danish Jihadist," August 29, 2014. www.thelocal.dk.

Quoted in Radio Free Europe, "Britain, Denmark, Belgium Join Fight Against IS in Iraq," September 26, 2014. www.rferl.org.

ranks of fighters growing, they feared the group posed a true military threat to their countries. In 2013 Iraqi president Nouri al-Maliki made a personal plea to President Obama for military aid, asking him to authorize drone strikes against ISIS positions. It would be a year, however, before Obama and other Western leaders pledged military assistance to defeat ISIS. By that time, ISIS had overrun the cities of Raqqa and Mosul and controlled thousands of square miles in Syria and Iraq.

The reason for Obama's reluctance to commit the American military to the fight against ISIS can be found in the decision by his predecessor, President George W. Bush, to invade Iraq a decade earlier. Since March 2003, when the US military led an invasion of Iraq to oust dictator Saddam Hussein, more than 1.5 million

US troops had served there. The war took a heavy toll on the troops: 4,500 soldiers lost their lives during the conflict, and another 30,000 suffered wounds, many returning home after losing limbs. Moreover, it was estimated that the US government had spent $1.7 trillion to execute the war.

During the years that US troops had been fighting in Iraq, a companion conflict had been waged in nearby Afghanistan, which the US military and its allies had invaded shortly after the September 11, 2001, terrorist attacks. The United States invaded Afghanistan to oust the Taliban, an Islamist regime that had seized control of the country during the 1990s. The United States had accused the Taliban of harboring the al Qaeda terrorists who planned and carried out the 2001 attacks.

As with the Iraq War, the conflict in Afghanistan had been costly in terms of human life. By 2011 nearly two thousand members of the American military had been killed in the war. Clearly,

Over two thousand US service personnel have been killed in operations in Afghanistan. The cost in lives has blunted America's commitment to fighting wars in the Middle East even if many Americans view terrorism from the region as a national threat.

due to the cost of the two wars in terms of human life, as well as their impacts on the national treasury, American citizens had grown weary of participating in armed conflicts in the Middle East.

Ending the wars in Iraq and Afghanistan had been a campaign promise made by Obama when the then-senator from Illinois ran for the presidency in 2008. After winning the election, Obama ordered gradual reductions in US troops in both wars. In December 2011 the last American troops left Iraq—just as ISIS was growing into a formidable military force. Yet as late as 2018, US troops were still engaged in Afghanistan.

A Troubling Report

Obama and other US officials had, in fact, known of the growing ISIS threat long before al-Maliki asked for drone strikes against ISIS positions. In the summer of 2012, the US Defense Intelligence Agency (DIA), which assesses military threats against the United States and its allies, had submitted a troubling report to the president. According to the DIA, the civil war in Syria, which started after the 2011 Arab Spring uprisings, had created a chaotic situation in that country. The DIA also raised serious doubts about the ability of the Iraqi government to maintain order in Iraq. Indeed, the report pointed out that al-Maliki—who had disbanded the Sunni militias following the Sunni Awakening—remained a very unpopular figure in Iraq. In the report, the DIA expressed fears of a rebirth of al Qaeda in Iraq or the continued rise of the Islamic State in that country. According to the DIA report,

> The deterioration of the situation [in Syria] has dire consequences on the Iraqi situation and . . . creates the ideal atmosphere for al-Qaeda in Iraq to return to its old pockets in Mosul . . . and will provide a renewed momentum under the presumption of unifying the jihad among Sunni Iraq and Syria, and the rest of the Sunnis in the Arab world against what it considers one enemy, the dissenters.

Islamic State in Iraq could also declare an Islamic State through union with other terrorist organizations in Iraq and Syria, which will create grave danger in regards to unifying Iraq and the protection of its territory . . . [and] renewing facilitation of terrorist elements from all over the Arab world entering into [the] Iraqi arena.[29]

Soon after the DIA report was issued, Obama convened a meeting of his top foreign policy advisers, including Secretary of State Hillary Clinton and Defense Secretary Leon Panetta. Clinton and Panetta backed a plan conceived by the US Central Intelligence Agency (CIA)—the nation's chief spy agency—to arm the rebels fighting against the government of Syrian president Bashar al-Assad with the understanding they would use the weapons against the Islamic State militants. Benjamin Rhodes, a deputy national security adviser, attended the meeting as well and recalled that the CIA plan was received coolly by Obama. "He was willing to consider options, but the question always was: 'What happens next?'" said Rhodes. "He did not see where a more interventionist military option led us, other than being deeper and deeper in a conflict that is extraordinarily complex and shows no signs of having a military solution."[30]

> "[President Obama] did not see where a more interventionist military option led us, other than being deeper and deeper in a conflict that is extraordinarily complex and shows no signs of having a military solution."[30]
>
> —Benjamin Rhodes, a deputy national security adviser

Clearly, Obama believed that providing arms to the Syrian rebels would be a first step toward drawing the United States deeper into the war against ISIS. This would require sending US troops back to the Middle East just months after Obama had withdrawn the final troops following eight years of combat in Iraq. Moreover, the CIA had offered the plan as Obama found himself in the midst of his campaign for reelection, meaning he was being asked to make the politically unpopular decision of recommitting US troops to Iraq, and perhaps even to Syria, while facing the voters. And so

Women Who Join ISIS

As many as six hundred women from America and Europe are believed to have left their homes to join ISIS. They are recruited in the same fashion as men, either radicalized by secret jihadist groups in their home countries or drawn into joining ISIS through social media.

Some women who join ISIS are raised in conservative Muslim homes where they are given little opportunity to travel or find new experiences away from their families. They see joining ISIS as an opportunity for adventure and a chance to travel far from home. "We talked to women who hadn't been radicalized but could understand why some of these girls might have gone to Syria and Iraq so they could live as 'good Muslims,'" says Emily Winterbotham, a researcher for the British Royal United Services Institute for Defence and Security Studies. "ISIS has been successful at selling that image to women. It's not just about the naïve vulnerable jihadi bride, it's women saying: 'This is in line with my religion, my political beliefs, the fact I want to live how I want.'"

Once they arrive in the Middle East, they are taken as brides by ISIS soldiers. Many, however, are expected to carry out acts of terrorism. One British woman, Sally Jones—a former guitarist for an all-girl rock band—converted to Islam and went by the name Umm Hussain al-Britani. By 2017 she was believed to be living in Iraq or Syria and had been implicated in two plots to kill Americans.

Quoted in Lizzie Dearden, "How ISIS Attracts Women and Girls from Europe with False Offer of 'Empowerment,'" *Independent* (London), August 5, 2017. www.independent.co.uk.

Obama turned down the plan. As Clinton explained, "The President had been elected in large part because of his opposition to the war in Iraq and his promise to bring the troops home. Getting entangled in any way in another sectarian civil war in the Middle East was not what he had in mind when coming into office."[31]

The Global Coalition to Defeat ISIS

More than two years later, Obama's attitude had changed. By the summer of 2014, ISIS had overrun Raqqa and Mosul, seizing control of a huge swath of territory in Iraq and Syria.

The publicized executions of prisoners had sent shock waves throughout the West. Evidence of the enslavement and murder of the Yazidis had also surfaced. The recruitment of jihadists from other Middle Eastern countries as well as Europe and America had continued. Clearly, world leaders believed that if ISIS was not defeated, the Islamic State would eventually export its brand of terrorism abroad. British prime minister David Cameron stated, "[ISIS] has oil, it has money, it has territory, it has weapons. And there's no doubt in my mind it has already undertaken and is planning further plots in Europe and elsewhere."[32]

In September 2014, forty nations announced the formation of the Global Coalition to Defeat ISIS with intentions to launch a military response against the Islamic State. (Eventually, the coalition grew to sixty-eight nations.) The coalition had the full support of the US government. In fact, it was built largely through the efforts of US secretary of state John Kerry, who had replaced Clinton in 2013. Obama said, "Our objective is clear: we will degrade, and

The Global Coalition on the Defeat of ISIS was formed to coordinate an armed response against ISIS. As a member, America has pledged chiefly to support partners in the region, impede the flow of foreign recruits, and stop enemy funding.

ultimately destroy, ISIL through a comprehensive and sustained counter-terrorism strategy. I will not hesitate to take action against ISIL in Syria, as well as Iraq. This is a core principle of my presidency: if you threaten America, you will find no safe haven."[33]

In announcing the formation of the Global Coalition, Obama acknowledged that there had not been a specific threat made by ISIS against the United States or other nations. But he pointed out that Americans and others should not wait for those threats to materialize. These nations needed to strike against ISIS before the group could organize attacks against them. Obama said, "Our intelligence community believes that thousands of foreigners—including Europeans and some Americans—have joined them in Syria and Iraq. Trained and battle-hardened, these fighters could try to return to their home countries and carry out deadly attacks."[34] Soon after joining the Global Coalition, the US military named its role in the mission Operation Inherent Resolve.

Obama had no intention of dispatching ground troops to Iraq and Syria. Nonetheless, he did send military instructors, tactical advisers, and, occasionally, special forces units for specific operations, such as freeing hostages or prisoners. Moreover, the US military agreed to provide arms and intelligence to the Iraqi government. Syria, however, was still led by Assad, who was regarded as a murderous despot by US officials. Therefore, although the United States would authorize air strikes against ISIS targets in Syria—as well as in Iraq—it would not provide arms and intelligence to Assad. The actual fighting on the ground would be carried out by the Iraqi and Syrian militaries and by ethnic militias in the two countries. Although the militias opposed their governments, they regarded ISIS as a common enemy. "I want the American people to understand how this effort will be different from the wars in Iraq and Afghanistan," Obama said. "It will not involve American combat troops fighting on foreign soil. This counter-terrorism campaign will be waged through a steady, relentless effort to take out ISIL wherever they exist using our air power and our support for partner forces on the ground."[35]

No American Boots on the Ground

In fact, the issue of sending US ground troops into the war against ISIS had been debated in Congress, with some members advocating the full use of the American military. During a hearing in 2014, Howard McKeon, a congressman from California and the chairman of the House Armed Services Committee, said the failure of the American military to fully commit to the fight could result in defeat. He insisted that Obama commit to using ground troops, if necessary, to defeat ISIS. "I will not support sending our military into harm's way with their arms tied behind their backs,"[36] declared McKeon.

> "I will not support sending our military into harm's way with their arms tied behind their backs."[36]
>
> —Howard McKeon, the chairman of the US House Armed Services Committee

Moreover, US Army general Martin E. Dempsey, the chairman of the Joint Chiefs of Staff and, therefore, the highest-ranking member of the American military, said he would also favor committing American ground troops to the conflict, if necessary. During a congressional hearing in 2014, he said, "If there are threats to the United States, then I, of course, would go back to the president and make a recommendation that may include the use of US military ground forces."[37]

But Obama stood steadfast in his resolve not to entangle US ground troops in another Middle Eastern conflict. In authorizing air strikes and the other measures—the use of instructors, tactical advisers, and special forces commandos—Obama employed a 2001 measure adopted by Congress that empowered the president to use military force against terrorists. Well into 2015, Congress debated the deployment of US ground troops to Iraq and Syria but ultimately could not agree on a plan. And so, as the war got under way against ISIS, it was largely conducted without the participation of American boots on the ground.

CHAPTER FOUR

Laying Siege to the Caliphate

In August 2015 a platoon of about thirty fighters allied with the Global Coalition to Defeat ISIS made its way through the streets of the Syrian city of Hasaka. Suddenly, the fighters found themselves under heavy fire from ISIS soldiers. They took cover, exchanging gunfire with the enemy. Clearly, the ISIS fire was coming from a building next to a green-domed mosque. Seeing the gunfire burst out of the building, a coalition fighter radioed the location of the building to fellow fighter Talal Raman, who was camped miles away.

Using the Google Earth app, Raman pinpointed the location of the building on a tablet computer, then relayed the position to an American military base hundreds of miles away. "Our comrades can see the enemy moving at the . . . address I just sent you,"[38] Raman wrote in a message to his American contact.

Raman transmitted the information to the Americans just after 10 p.m. At 10:12 p.m., his American contact asked for confirmation that the coalition unit in Hasaka was still under fire. Raman replied that his comrades were still under attack. "Is there a fighter jet overhead?" he asked his contact. "Yes, and they're preparing to strike,"[39] the contact replied.

At 10:23 p.m., Raman received a message on his tablet that included a Google Earth map with a yellow circle drawn about 100 yards (91 m) north of the ISIS target. The message instructed Raman to tell the coalition fighters to retreat to the area in the yellow circle. Raman passed on the information. A few minutes later, Raman was asked to confirm that the coalition fighters had retreated. "The pilot is waiting,"[40] the message said. Raman radioed the fighters in the field, who confirmed they had made it to the yellow zone. Raman relayed the information to the Americans.

At 10:38 p.m., Raman received a new message from the Americans: the air strike would commence in three minutes. As the minutes ticked by, he continued to receive follow-up messages counting down to the strike.

Back in Hasaka, the coalition fighters watched as the building containing the ISIS fighters suddenly exploded—struck by a missile fired from the US jet overhead. The coalition fighters left the yellow zone and made their way to the scene. In the rubble, they found the bodies of nine ISIS soldiers.

A Decisive Defeat at Kobani

The mission in Hasaka illustrated how much of the war against ISIS was waged. On the ground, coalition fighters made their way through the streets of ISIS-held cities. Upon confronting ISIS soldiers, the fighters were assisted in their assaults by air strikes launched by the United States and other coalition members, including the United Kingdom, France, Australia, Germany, and Canada. Several Middle Eastern nations, among them Saudi Arabia and Jordan, joined the coalition as well and provided air support for the ground assaults.

Two years earlier, when ISIS fighters had swept through a number of Syrian and Iraqi cities, they proved themselves to be relentless fighters. Now, unlike their opponents, ISIS was forced to wage war without air support—ISIS lacked jets, helicopters, drones, and missiles. Nor did ISIS have access to spy satellites orbiting overhead, relaying valuable intelligence to military commanders below.

As for the coalition fighters on the ground, many—like Raman and his comrades—were members of an ethnic group known as Kurds. The Kurds were not soldiers in the Iraqi or Syrian armies; they were members of citizen militias that played vital roles in the war against ISIS. The Kurds took up arms against ISIS because they had much to fear from the Islamic State—some 30 million Kurds live in Iraq, Syria, and other Middle Eastern countries.

An elite unit of female Kurdish soldiers trains outside Baghdad, Iraq, to fight Islamist militants. Although Muslim, the Kurds place fewer restrictions on women, allowing them to hold jobs, leave their heads uncovered, and serve in military forces.

Although most Kurds are Muslims, ISIS found little regard for them, believing their customs to be too liberal. For example, Kurdish people are known to practice other faiths, such as Christianity and Judaism, which would never be accepted by ISIS. Moreover, Muslim Kurdish women need not cover their faces when they are in public; they are also permitted to attend school, hold jobs, and serve in elected office. They may also join the military and serve as soldiers, even commanding units in the field. Such freedoms would never be permitted under ISIS.

In fact, the Kurds proved themselves to be hardened fighters. Shortly after the offensive against ISIS commenced in 2014, Kurdish fighters participated in the first significant victory scored by the coalition against ISIS. That fall, the United States and other members began a bombing campaign against ISIS positions in the Syrian city of Kobani, located near the country's border with Turkey. From September through January, coalition aircraft staged some seven hundred air strikes against ISIS positions in

Air Strikes and the Civilian Toll

The Global Coalition to Defeat ISIS staged nearly thirty thousand air strikes against ISIS, deploying drones, jet fighters, and Vietnam War–era B-52 bombers. Although the strikes accomplished their goal—assisting the ground troops in the ultimate victory over ISIS—civilians suffered during the aerial attacks.

Whole neighborhoods in Iraqi and Syrian cities were obliterated. In Mosul, approximately ten thousand civilians lost their lives, many dying during the air assaults. One Mosul resident, Basim Razzo, had owned a comfortable home on the banks of the Tigris River. His family had been asleep on the night of September 20, 2015, when Razzo suddenly snapped awake to an atmosphere of thick dust. Blinking through the dust, he found no roof overhead. His house had been hit by a coalition missile, which killed his wife, Mayada, and daughter, Tuqa. Also destroyed in the blast was the house next door, which was occupied by his brother Mohannad and his family. Mohannad and his son Najib were killed in the blast. "In the middle of the night, Coalition airplanes targeted two houses occupied by innocent civilians," Razzo said. "Is this technology? This barbarian attack cost the lives of my wife, daughter, brother and nephew."

Following the strike, coalition officials defended the attack. "US and Coalition forces work very hard to be precise in airstrikes," said Shane Huff, a spokesperson for the US military. "[The Coalition] is conducting one of the most precise air campaigns in military history." Despite this precision, faulty intelligence had mistaken the Razzo home for an ISIS bomb-making factory.

Quoted in Azmat Khan and Anand Gopal, "The Uncounted," *New York Times Magazine*, November 16, 2017. www.nytimes.com.

and near Kobani. Intelligence had identified nearly three hundred ISIS positions in and around the city, which were targeted by the coalition air strikes. Certainly, though, these strikes took a heavy toll on the city: more than one hundred buildings were destroyed in the attacks. Also, many civilians were known to have died in the siege as well.

But ISIS paid the highest toll. As the air strikes intensified, ISIS commanders dispatched reinforcements to the city. By late January, some three thousand ISIS fighters were believed to have been killed either through air strikes or during street-to-street combat against the Kurdish militias. Finally, on January 26, 2015, coalition leaders declared victory in Kobani. "Nobody is declaring any sort of strategic turning point or anything like that," a coalition spokesperson said. "However, in terms of the early phase of this multiyear campaign, we see Kobani as significant. That's why we are encouraged by the trends we're seeing now. . . . The fact that ISIL poured thousands of fighters into Kobani and failed—it is a decisive defeat."[41]

Commando Strike

In addition to the Kurds, other regional forces also took up arms against ISIS. The Syrian Democratic Forces was a group of rebels who had been fighting to depose Syrian president Bashar al-Assad since the Arab Spring of 2011. Now, though, they had been persuaded to fight against ISIS, recognizing that the Islamic State posed as much of a threat to the Syrian people as Assad did. Moreover, the soldiers of the Iraqi army—who two years earlier had turned and run in the face of the ISIS assault—were now undergoing training by military advisers from the United States and other coalition states. Soon, the Iraqi army would be retrained into a viable fighting force and sent into battle against ISIS. Syrian soldiers under Assad eventually joined the battle as well.

Under President Obama's orders, however, no US ground troops were deployed to the areas controlled by the Islamic State except for special forces commandos sent into the field for specific, limited missions. These commandos were given their first mission in May 2015, when CIA intelligence led them to a house occupied by Abu Sayyaf, a close associate of ISIS leader Abu Bakr al-Baghdadi. Abu Sayyaf headed the ISIS oil-exporting program, a valuable source of income for the Islamic State. "He managed the oil infrastructure and financial generation details for ISIL," a coalition official explained. "Given that job, he was pretty well-connected."[42]

ISIS's control over oil-producing parts of Iraq and Syria has allowed it to hijack wells and production. The stolen oil ends up being sold throughout the region or smuggled into neighboring countries.

In the early morning hours of May 16, twenty-four members of the US Army's crack Delta Force commando unit were flown by helicopters to the Syrian city of Amr, landing near a home occupied by Abu Sayyaf. As they approached the house, they encountered fire from his bodyguards. They fought through the resistance, killing about a dozen ISIS fighters.

Delta Force's mission was to take Abu Sayyaf captive so that he could be interrogated by intelligence agents, who hoped to draw valuable information from the ISIS official. They found Abu Sayyaf in the home, but he drew a weapon on the Americans and was instantly killed by commando fire. The commandos did take his wife as a prisoner. They also found an eighteen-year-old Yazidi woman in the home. She had been kept as a slave by Abu Sayyaf. The woman was freed and returned to the coalition base with the commandos; she was eventually reunited with her family.

Although Abu Sayyaf was killed in the raid, coalition officials hoped his wife could still provide valuable intelligence about ISIS, such as the names and whereabouts of other leaders. Either way, an important ISIS leader—an official responsible for raising cash for the Islamic State through oil sales—had now been eliminated. This was certain to impede ISIS fighters as they found themselves waging war with dwindling financial resources.

Operation Tidal Wave II

Cutting off ISIS's oil revenue had, in fact, been a priority for the coalition soon after the fighting started in late 2014. ISIS had been earning as much as $50 million a month in oil sales. By 2017, however, coalition officials announced that they had been successful in cutting the Islamic State's oil exports by as much as 90 percent.

The coalition employed air strikes to knock out tanker trucks. Within two years, these air strikes had destroyed more than two thousand trucks, which ISIS used to ferry oil from the desert oil fields to port cities. Pipelines and other oil infrastructure were also targeted. The coalition named this campaign Operation Tidal Wave II. The original Operation Tidal Wave had been waged during World War II by the Allied forces to stem the flow of oil that fueled the ships, tanks, and planes of the German military. Operation Tidal Wave II targeted oil fields in Iraq and Syria, particularly the oil-rich Deir al-Zour region in eastern Syria, which was under ISIS control.

Oil was not the only source of revenue that helped the Islamic State obtain arms and control its territory. Banks in cities taken over by ISIS were looted. Also, people living in the Islamic State were taxed. But as the coalition moved against ISIS, liberating cities from the group's control, ISIS

> "Their territory is shrinking and so is their ability to tax people."[43]
>
> —Andrew Tabler, an analyst at the Institute for Near East Policy

found its tax revenue shrinking because the group was able to bleed taxes out of fewer and fewer people. By 2017, experts estimated that the loss of oil and tax revenue had cut the ISIS treasury in half. "Losing half their revenues means a lot," said Andrew Tabler, an analyst at the Institute for Near East Policy, a Washington, DC, group that studies US-Mideast relations. "Their territory is shrinking and so is their ability to tax people."[43]

Cutting Off the Weapons Trade

With its sources of revenue drying up, ISIS found it increasingly difficult to buy weapons and pay its soldiers. When ISIS first seized control of territory, the group was able to obtain many weapons by capturing them from members of the Iraqi and Syrian armies. (These arms were primarily supplied by manufacturers in the United States, which supported the Iraqi government, and Russia, which backed the Assad regime in Syria.) However, once the military campaign against ISIS ramped up in late 2014 and early 2015, ISIS was forced to turn to the murky world of the underground arms trade to buy guns and ammunition.

After the war commenced, many of the weapons and the ammunition that made it into ISIS hands were supplied by arms manufacturers in eastern Europe. Ironically, these shipments were arranged by the CIA. They were supposed to have been supplied to the Syrian Democratic Forces and other groups rebelling against Assad, but instead they found their way into the hands of ISIS fighters. The arms had been diverted along the way by smugglers who were willing to sell the weapons to the highest bidders—in this case, ISIS.

When it became clear that ISIS was obtaining weapons meant for the Syrian Democratic Forces, the CIA stepped in and stopped the arms shipments. "If you supply weapons and ammunition . . . in a very complex interlocked conflict then the risk of diversion is very, very high,"[44] said James Bevan, who headed a team from Conflict Armament Research, a British-based group that tracks the international illegal arms trade.

> "If you supply weapons and ammunition . . . in a very complex interlocked conflict then the risk of diversion is very, very high."[44]
>
> —James Bevan, a weapons investigator for Conflict Armament Research

The Battle to Liberate Mosul

With its source of weapons and oil revenue virtually cut off, by 2016 ISIS found its ability to wage war greatly hampered. More-

Saudi Arabia's Fears

Although led by a Sunni regime, Saudi Arabia felt threatened by ISIS. The Saudis are custodians of some of Islam's holiest sites, among them the Kaaba shrine in the Saudi city of Mecca. Each year, tens of thousands of Muslims make a pilgrimage known as the hajj—a journey to Mecca to worship at the Kaaba. According to the Koran, Muslims must make the hajj at least once in their lifetimes. The Saudis feared that the establishment of the ISIS caliphate would delegitimize their role as guardian of Islam's holy sites.

Saudi Arabia shares a 600-mile-long (966 km) border with Iraq. During the war against ISIS, gunfire often erupted along the border. After joining the Global Coalition to Defeat ISIS, the Saudis mainly provided air support to the ground troops as well as financial support and weapons to the ethnic militias fighting the Islamic State. "ISIS presents itself as the 'authentic Islamic caliphate,' and that of course presents Saudi Arabia with a religious challenge, because the Saudi state is the custodian of the holy sites of Islam," says Lina Khatib, a Middle East analyst at Chatham House, a British agency that studies international relations. "The problem that Saudi Arabia has with ISIS is beyond terrorism and instability. It's also about the ideological challenge and competition that the Islamic State project poses."

Quoted in Priyanka Boghani and Anjali Tsui, "Who's Who in the Fight Against ISIS?," *Frontline*, PBS, October 11, 2016. www.pbs.org.

over, the relentless assaults by coalition air strikes and the street-by-street fighting on the ground had taken their toll, shrinking the territory under control of the Islamic State.

Coalition troops moved into areas controlled by the Islamic State, winning back territory that had been lost to the group in 2014. By the spring of 2016 the Iraqi army had recaptured the cities of Hit, Rutbah, and Fallujah. By the fall, Iraqi troops and the Kurdish militias were poised to begin an assault on Mosul. With a population of some 2.5 million people, Mosul was the largest city under ISIS control.

The battle lasted for months. ISIS and coalition forces fought street by street, and coalition air strikes rained down missiles on

The Rise and Fall of ISIS

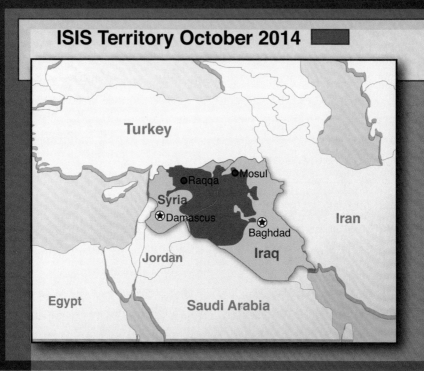

ISIS Territory October 2014

Turkey

Raqqa ● Mosul

Syria

Damascus

Iran

Baghdad

Iraq

Jordan

Egypt

Saudi Arabia

ISIS Territory October 2017

Turkey

Raqqa ● Mosul

Syria

Damascus

Iran

Baghdad

Iraq

Jordan

Egypt

Saudi Arabia

the ISIS positions. Complicating the mission was the ISIS strategy of embedding its fighters among civilians and waging attacks from residential streets. Therefore, an air strike targeting the enemy would also likely wipe out innocent civilians. By the spring of 2017, as the battle neared its conclusion, ISIS kidnapped hundreds of civilians and forced them into an area of Mosul known as the Old City—a heavily congested warren of narrow streets along the banks of the Tigris River. As American journalist Ivor Prockett observed,

> "Some of the soldiers here, as well as one resident who had managed to flee, spoke of the Islamic State fighters' trying to round up anyone still living in the area and forcing them to retreat with them toward the Old City."[45]
>
> —Journalist Ivor Prockett

> Ahead lies Mosul's Old City, and perhaps the worst fight yet. As the battle has drawn closer to that area's tight and jagged streets, the number of fleeing civilians has dropped sharply.
>
> Some of the soldiers here, as well as one resident who had managed to flee, spoke of the Islamic State fighters' trying to round up anyone still living in the area and forcing them to retreat with them toward the Old City.
>
> It's a chilling thought, horrifyingly consistent with how the Islamic State has fought this battle for months. The militants' last stand may well take place behind a wall of civilians.[45]

The Siege of Raqqa

As the battle raged to liberate Mosul, coalition troops moved through Syria as well. Moreover, by 2017 Assad had redirected some of his troops away from the ongoing fight against revolutionaries to the war against ISIS. Therefore, ISIS found itself facing a new foe—the Syrian army.

The climactic battle against ISIS in Syria was waged in Raqqa, a city of some two hundred thousand people. Kurdish militias and the Syrian Democratic Forces carried the fight into the streets. But as in Mosul, ISIS embedded its fighters in residential neighborhoods, costing many civilian lives.

In October 2017, coalition forces declared victory in both Raqqa and Mosul. Civilian casualties were high: an estimated ten thousand civilians lost their lives in Mosul, and about two thousand civilians were killed in Raqqa.

For the next several weeks, coalition forces continued to search for ISIS fighters in Syria and Iraq. Finally, on December 9, 2017, Iraqi officials declared victory over ISIS. "All Iraqi lands are liberated from terrorist Daesh gangs and our forces completely control the international Iraqi-Syrian border,"[46] said Abdul-Amir Rasheed Yar Allah, a general in the Iraqi army. Syrian leaders also declared that ISIS fighters had been defeated in their country.

Three years after ISIS swept through territory in Syria and Iraq, the armies and civilian militias of the Middle East, along with the formidable coalition air forces, were able to defeat the organization. In its quest to establish a caliphate based on seventh-century traditions, ISIS had been defeated by weapons and tactics developed for twenty-first-century warfare. But as ISIS fighters streamed out of Iraq and Syria, they found havens in other Middle Eastern nations, vowing that their mission was not yet over.

CHAPTER FIVE

The War Continues

On December 10, 2017—just two days after Iraqi leaders declared victory over ISIS—Akayed Ullah strapped a homemade bomb to his body and attempted to detonate the device in a subway station beneath Times Square in New York City. The attempt failed when the bomb malfunctioned—causing minor injuries to three people nearby but inflicting significant burns to the bomber's abdomen.

Ullah, a twenty-seven-year-old immigrant from the Asian nation of Bangladesh, was hospitalized after the bombing attempt. As he recovered in the hospital, police learned that Ullah had immigrated to America in 2011. He held a US permanent resident card, better known as a green card because of the greenish tint of the document. Issued by the US Citizenship and Immigration Services, a green card permits its holder to remain in America indefinitely. Many green card holders eventually apply for US citizenship.

Ullah lived in the New York City borough of Brooklyn and worked as an electrician. Hasan Alam, a former neighbor of Ullah's in Brooklyn, said he never regarded Ullah as being capable of violence. "I'm actually very shocked," Alam said. "Because he was a religious person and very quiet, not very outgoing."[47] Another former neighbor added, "The family is very friendly, very nice, but he was quiet. Never talked to anyone, stayed to himself."[48]

But when police interviewed Ullah, he told them he was inspired to commit the act of terrorism by ISIS and had fully expected to die in the explosion. As Ullah followed the news of the war on ISIS, he found himself sympathizing with the ISIS soldiers who were under assault by the relentless air attacks by the United States and other Global Coalition members. The attack beneath Times Square, he said, was staged to avenge the ISIS soldiers

Well-armed police units patrol the streets of New York after Akayed Ullah, an ISIS-inspired suicide bomber, detonated a homemade device in a subway station below Times Square in 2017. Fortunately, the bomb only partially exploded, injuring Ullah and three individuals nearby.

who had lost their lives in the coalition air strikes. "I did it for the Islamic State," Ullah told police. Moreover, when police looked through the bomber's passport, they found this handwritten note by Ullah: "O America, die in your rage."[49]

Ullah remained in custody in 2018, awaiting trial on the charges of criminal possession of a weapon, support for an act of terrorism, and making a terroristic threat. If convicted of all charges, he faces a maximum sentence of life in prison.

Lone Wolves

After investigating Ullah, police concluded that the bomber had never made contact with ISIS; he had never visited territory controlled by the Islamic State and, therefore, had never undergone training in how to fashion the bomb or how to pick a target that would cause the most death and destruction. In fact, the bomb concocted by Ullah was crude in its construction, a major factor in why it failed to fully detonate and kill or significantly injure anyone other than himself.

Still, there is no question that ISIS and its campaign against twenty-first-century Western culture was a significant factor in Ullah's decision to carry out the act of terrorism. Such perpetrators of terrorism are known as lone wolves. They act alone, without training or any other assistance from ISIS, but are nevertheless inspired to commit acts of terror by ISIS and its ultimate goal of establishing a Middle Eastern caliphate.

Other attacks by lone-wolf terrorists had been perpetrated before ISIS attempted to establish its caliphate in 2014. For several years many lone wolves had committed attacks on innocent people in support of other terrorist groups, including al Qaeda. When ISIS emerged, it openly encouraged lone-wolf attacks and was quick to take credit for inspiring the acts of violence after they occurred. In 2015, as ISIS found itself under siege by the Global Coalition, an ISIS spokesperson called for supporters in the United States and other Western countries to

> "I did it for the Islamic State."[49]
>
> —Akayed Ullah, a failed suicide bomber in New York City

commit violent acts in their homelands. According to the spokesperson, "The smallest action you do in the heart of their land is dearer to us than the largest action by us and more effective and more damaging to them."[50]

New Yorkers avoided serious injury during Ullah's attack, but others have not been so fortunate. Indeed, since 2014 authorities report at least a dozen attacks on US soil that have been inspired by ISIS. On November 29, 2016, Abdul Razak Ali Artan, an immigrant from the African nation of Somalia, perpetrated an attack on the campus of Ohio State University in Columbus. Artan rammed his car into a crowd of people. He then exited the car and slashed his victims with a knife. Eleven people were injured, but none sustained a life-threatening wound. Artan was shot and killed by police during the attack.

Another ISIS-inspired attack occurred on December 2, 2015, when twenty-eight-year-old Syed Rizwan Farook and his wife, twenty-seven-year-old Tashfeen Malik, entered a government building in San Bernardino, California, and began shooting, killing fourteen people and wounding twenty-one others. Farook was a US citizen, born in Chicago to parents who had emigrated from Pakistan; his wife was an immigrant from Pakistan. They escaped from the scene but were chased down by police and killed in a barrage of gunfire on a nearby street.

As horrific as the San Bernardino incident may have been, it was not the worst ISIS-inspired attack to have occurred on US soil. On June 12, 2016, twenty-nine-year-old Omar Mateen, a US citizen who was born in New York City to parents who had emigrated from Afghanistan, entered a nightclub in Orlando, Florida. He began shooting a semiautomatic weapon, eventually killing forty-nine people before police made their way into the club and killed the terrorist. During the attack, Mateen made a cell phone call to police, pledging his allegiance to ISIS.

Attacks in Europe

ISIS has inspired attacks in other countries as well. In September 2017, twenty-nine people were injured when a bomb exploded in a subway station in London. That attack came five months after twenty-nine people were killed by a suicide bomber in the British city of Manchester while attending a concert by singer Ariana Grande. In June 2017, a truck driven by a jihadist killed eight and injured nearly fifty people as it drove into pedestrians crossing London Bridge. In December 2016 a truck plowed into a pedestrian market in Berlin, Germany, killing twelve and injuring forty-eight. In France, a gunman killed a policeman and wounded two others in April 2017. He was shot and killed by police. The incident occurred in Paris, along the internationally famous boulevard known as the Champs-Élysées. In all cases, ISIS claimed responsibility for inspiring the terrorists to kill innocent civilians.

Defeating ISIS Online

ISIS recruited fighters through social media, radicalizing them through posts on Facebook, Twitter, and other Internet platforms. Now that the Islamic State has been defeated on the ground, the Global Coalition to Defeat ISIS is working toward eliminating ISIS messages on social media.

The Global Coalition established the Communications Working Group, which consists of representatives from the United States, the United Kingdom, and the United Arab Emirates. The group uses software that identifies incendiary social media messages from ISIS. Once the messages are identified, the group reaches out to a network of activists who respond online by pointing out the falsehoods of the posts.

One of those activists is Abdalaziz Alhamza, who lives in the Syrian city of Raqqa. Alhamza and several friends risked their lives by responding to ISIS's social media posts even while ISIS occupied Raqqa. Alhamza explains,

> [We] wanted the rest of the world to know what was happening in our home town, so we snuck covert footage and photos out of the city, publishing them on social media and ultimately sending to various news organizations to show that Raqqa was not the utopia that ISIS claimed. Now, when people search for Raqqa on the Internet, instead of finding ISIS propaganda, they find our website listing the abuses carried out by ISIS. . . . We must continue to fight against the ideology of ISIS. Our group works diligently to point out the hypocrisy and the lies of ISIS' media campaign—an act of resistance that the terror group does not like.

Quoted in Abdalaziz Alhamza, "Bombs Will Not Defeat ISIS (but Maybe the Internet Will)," *New York Times*, July 6, 2017. www.nytimes.com.

Officials concede there is little that can be done to prevent lone-wolf attacks. If a terrorist cell spends months planning an attack, recruiting followers and obtaining weapons, law enforcement agencies have a better chance to learn about the plot through informants and surveillance than they do if a single person decides on his or her own to commit an act of terror. "[It is] almost impossible to detect that, unless they open up about their feelings to family and friends,"[51] says Matthew Heiman, a former attorney for the US Justice Department. That explains why in Ullah's case, his friends and neighbors were shocked to learn he had attempted to explode a bomb—he had never told anybody of his intentions.

Even without informants, there are actions local police can take to help prevent terrorism. For instance, in the days leading up to major public occasions—such as sporting events, concerts, or parades—they will step up patrols and initiate checkpoint searches. For example, people attending the annual Macy's Thanksgiving Day Parade in New York City in 2017 had to submit to police inspections of handbags, backpacks, and similar parcels at checkpoints set up in the city's Central Park. Clearly, police were searching for hidden bombs. New York police commissioner James O'Neill said the inspections were in response to the terror acts in Orlando, Columbus, and San Bernardino. "We had a couple of tough months as a nation," O'Neill said. "We

NYPD officers search bags at a checkpoint where pedestrians access the 2017 Macy's Thanksgiving Day Parade route. Because of the threat of suicide bombings or other terrorist acts, major cities boost police presence at events that attract large crowds.

won't ever accept such acts of hate and cowardice as inevitable in our society."[52]

The Travel Ban

In January and March 2017, newly elected US president Donald Trump took action that he said was intended to protect Americans from terrorist attacks. He signed executive orders banning travel to the United States by people from several countries, including Syria, Chad, Iran, Libya, Somalia, and Yemen—nations where he believed jihadists were most active.

Civil libertarians, however, contend that the ban specifically targets Muslims. Therefore, it violates the US Constitution, which guarantees the freedom of religion. "This new executive order is nothing more than [a] Muslim ban," said Douglas Chin, the attorney general of Hawaii. "Under the pretense of national security, it still targets immigrants and refugees. It leaves the door open for even further restrictions."[53] Hawaii was one of several states with large immigrant populations that challenged the ban in court.

> "This new executive order is nothing more than [a] Muslim ban."[53]
>
> —Douglas Chin, attorney general of Hawaii

Throughout 2017 the ban faced numerous court tests. In late 2017 the US Supreme Court permitted the ban to be implemented pending the outcomes of challenges filed in the lower courts. The Supreme Court was expected to await lower court decisions before making a final ruling—sometime in 2018.

Other countries that have been victimized by terrorist attacks have not reacted by banning immigration. However, they have introduced measures such as banning people living in their countries from traveling to other countries for the purpose of joining jihadist movements. Many countries have also tightened laws banning people from encouraging acts of terrorism as well as imposing lengthy prison sentences on anyone found guilty of doing so or of actually participating in terror plots.

An ISIS Resurgence

ISIS has taken credit for inspiring numerous terrorist acts across the globe. Yet by late 2017 the Islamic State's occupation of territory had ceased to exist. With victories over ISIS declared by the governments of Iraq and Syria, ISIS has evolved into a confederation of terrorists who must resort to underground methods to meet, share information, and plan their next moves. Prior to the Global Coalition's war against ISIS, intelligence officers estimated that about forty thousand fighters had traveled to Iraq and Syria from the United States, Europe, and several Middle Eastern nations to join the group. Now that the ground war has ended, officials fear that acts of terrorism may eventually go beyond the lone-wolf attacks if former ISIS fighters are able to regroup and launch attacks on a wider scale. Of those forty thousand fighters, about fifty-six hundred are believed to have made their way home after the fighting ended in Mosul and Raqqa. Many others are believed to have been killed in the fighting or captured by the Iraqi and Syrian militaries; by early 2018, however, no estimate had been placed on that number. Still other fighters are believed to have fled to Libya, Turkey, Afghanistan, and the Philippines.

All of these former ISIS fighters are believed to represent a significant threat. According to a 2017 report by the New York–based Soufan Group, a private company that provides security training to corporations and national governments, "As the territorial caliphate shrinks and is increasingly denied an overt presence, its leadership will look to supporters overseas, including returnees, to keep the brand alive."[54]

Moreover, experts believe world leaders should be wary of the possibility that ISIS can regroup and try again to form a caliphate. Indeed, experts point out that the fate of ISIS leader Abu Bakr al-Baghdadi has never been determined; thus, he may still be alive and in hiding, planning to lead a resurgence of ISIS.

If there were to be a resurgence by ISIS, intelligence experts fear it could involve ISIS-affiliated terrorist cells, not just lone wolves. On December 28, 2017, just days after the governments

Reaching Out to Prison Inmates

Officials in France determined that many jihadists are former prison inmates who were radicalized while they were incarcerated. Typically, the French found, the inmates had been jailed for minor crimes, such as petty theft. Once inside, though, the inmates came into contact with Islamists who radicalized them, winning them over to jihadism. According to French officials, when these minor criminals had finished out their sentences, many left France and traveled to Iraq and Syria, where they joined ISIS and became soldiers for the Islamic State.

The French have taken numerous steps to prevent this from happening. For starters, they are working very hard to identify incarcerated Islamists and separate them from the general prison populations. These Islamists are then provided counseling with prison psychologists and others who attempt to deradicalize them, changing their ideas about the mission of Islam in the twenty-first century. Many moderate Muslim clerics have also been hired to meet with incarcerated jihadists to help reeducate them. As Mourad Benchellali, a former French jihadist who spent four years in prison, explains, "If you put all these people together who are only thinking about radical Islam, who are only talking about it, it's hard to break that mentality." He now speaks with incarcerated inmates in French prisons, helping them moderate their views.

Law enforcement authorities have also been active in prisons. In 2016 the French government disclosed that it had assigned 185 undercover officers to work inside prisons. These officers have posed as inmates in order to gather intelligence and better identify jihadists likely to radicalize other inmates.

Quoted in Brandon A. Patterson, "French Prisons May Be Producing Dangerous Terrorists: Here's What America Can Learn from That," *Mother Jones*, August 1, 2016. www.motherjones.com.

of Iraq and Syria declared victory over ISIS, a terrorist group in Afghanistan staged an attack on a Shia cultural center in the capital city of Kabul. The attack, which killed forty-one people and injured eighty-four others, was carried out by a suicide bomber. A group affiliated with ISIS known as Wilayah Khorasan took responsibility for the attack. *Wilayah Khorasan* means "Khorasan province," a fifteen-hundred-year-old name that ISIS uses to refer to Afghanistan. The group is also known as ISIS-K.

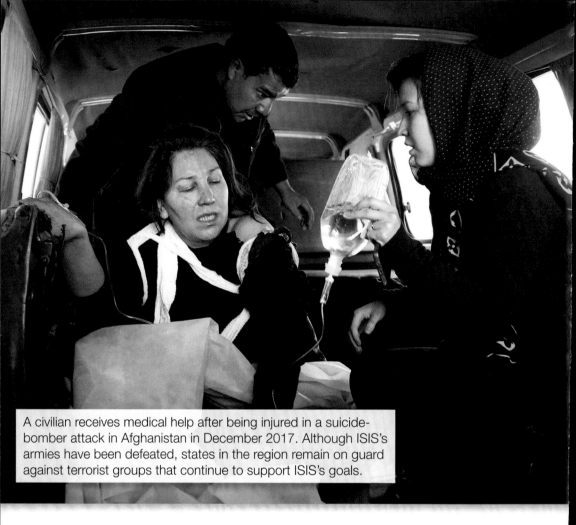

A civilian receives medical help after being injured in a suicide-bomber attack in Afghanistan in December 2017. Although ISIS's armies have been defeated, states in the region remain on guard against terrorist groups that continue to support ISIS's goals.

Meanwhile, in the United Kingdom, the Intelligence and Security Committee of Parliament issued a report in late 2017 predicting that ISIS intends to sponsor terrorist acts targeting British citizens. "The scale of the current threat facing [the United Kingdom] and its interests from Islamist terror groups is unprecedented," the committee reported. "This threat is predominantly driven by the activities of [ISIS] in Syria and Iraq, which seeks to maintain the group's image and narrative of success in the face of military losses."[55]

An Incomplete Victory

Experts also point out that the conditions that led to the Islamic State's creation in 2014 have not changed. Rebels in Syria are still fighting against the government of Syrian president Bashar al-Assad. In Iraq, the Kurds have long desired an autonomous homeland. Kurdish fighters, who fought against ISIS alongside Iraqi troops, have already turned against the Iraqis and have traded gunfire with their former allies. Such instability in Iraq and Syria could again leave open the possibility that ISIS will regroup and take advantage of the chaos to seize territory. Experts point out that many remote parts of Iraq and Syria can certainly harbor ISIS soldiers. There, they can regroup and obtain weapons far from the scrutiny of the Iraqi and Syrian militaries.

> "The scale of the current threat facing [the United Kingdom] and its interests from Islamist terror groups is unprecedented."[55]
>
> —The British Parliament's Intelligence and Security Committee

Political scientists Benjamin Bahney and Patrick B. Johnston argue that ISIS will attempt to spark dissent and violence between Sunni and Shiite Muslims, leading many Sunnis to believe that ISIS is their only hope for protection against Shiites. Writing for the RAND Corporation, a California-based organization that studies foreign policy, Johnston and Bahney contend that

> the victory [over ISIS] is incomplete—and not just when it comes to the challenges of ISIS-inspired lone-wolf attacks, foreign fighters returning home from Iraq and Syria, and the persistence of ISIS franchises elsewhere. While such concerns are real, a more dangerous scenario also deserves some attention: ISIS could resurrect its caliphate where it was born, in Iraq and Syria.[56]

As leaders of the United States and European nations remain vigilant against terrorism on their home soil, they must watch as the fractured nations of Iraq and Syria attempt to rebuild their societies in the wake of the victory over ISIS. If Syria and Iraq fail to establish peaceful and secure societies, ISIS or similar groups know from experience they can easily gain a foothold and wreak havoc across wide swaths of the Middle East.

SOURCE NOTES

Introduction: ISIS: A Threat to Global Security

1. Benjamin Hall, *Inside ISIS: The Brutal Rise of a Terrorist Army*. New York: Center Street, 2015. Kindle edition.
2. Quoted in Jessica Stern and J.M. Berger, *ISIS: The State of Terror*. New York: HarperCollins, 2015, p. 121.
3. Malcolm Nance, *Defeating ISIS: Who They Are, How They Fight, What They Believe*. New York: Skyhorse, 2016, p. xix.
4. Quoted in David Hudson, "Barack Obama: 'We Will Degrade and Ultimately Destroy ISIL,'" Obama White House Archives, September, 10, 2014. https://obamawhitehouse.archives.gov.
5. Quoted in Andrew Sparrow, "PM Returns from Holiday After Video Shows US Reporter Beheaded by Briton," *Guardian* (Manchester, UK), August 20, 2014. www.theguardian.com.

Chapter One: The Rise of ISIS

6. William McCants, *The ISIS Apocalypse: The History, Strategy, and Doomsday Vision of the Islamic State*. New York: St. Martin's, 2015, p. 10.
7. Quoted in BBC News, "Islamic State: 'Baghdadi Message' Issued by Jihadists," November 13, 2014. www.bbc.com.
8. Quoted in Joby Warrick, *Black Flags: The Rise of ISIS*. New York: Doubleday, 2015, p. 244.
9. Quoted in Warrick, *Black Flags*, p. 244.
10. Quoted in Warrick, *Black Flags*, pp. 251–52.
11. Quoted in Warrick, *Black Flags*, p. 283.
12. Quoted in Graeme Wood, "What ISIS Really Wants," *Atlantic*, March 2015. www.theatlantic.com.
13. Richard Engel, *And Then All Hell Broke Loose: Two Decades in the Middle East*. New York: Simon & Schuster, 2016, pp. 193–94.
14. Quoted in Warrick, *Black Flags*, p. 305.

Chapter Two: Life Under ISIS

15. Farida Khalaf and Andrea C. Hoffman, *The Girl Who Escaped ISIS: This Is My Story*. New York: ATRIA, 2016, p. 87.

16. Khalaf and Hoffman, *The Girl Who Escaped ISIS*, p. 219.
17. Quoted in Wood, "What ISIS Really Wants."
18. Quoted in *Economist*, "Islam and Slavery: The Persistence of History," August 22, 2015. www.economist.com.
19. Salam al-Marayati, "No, ISIS Doesn't Represent Islam," CNN, September 2, 2015. www.cnn.com.
20. Quoted in Derek Stoffel, "Life Under ISIS: Mosul Residents Reflect on a Brutal Occupation," CBC News, March 22, 2017. www.cbc.ca.
21. Quoted in Patrick Cockburn Karbala, "Isis in Mosul: Brutal Metal Instrument Used to Clip Women's Flesh Shows Increasing Barbarity Within 'Caliphate's' Own Walls," *Independent* (London), February 25, 2016. www.independent.co.uk.
22. Quoted in Karbala, "Isis in Mosul."
23. Nance, *Defeating ISIS*, p. 253.
24. Nance, *Defeating ISIS*, p. 255.
25. Quoted in Fazel Hawramy, Shalaw Mohammed, and Kareem Shaheen, "Life Under Isis in Raqqa and Mosul: 'We're Living in a Giant Prison,'" *Guardian* (Manchester, UK), December 9, 2015. www.theguardian.com.
26. Quoted in Hawramy, Mohammed, and Shaheen, "Life Under Isis in Raqqa and Mosul."

Chapter Three: The Path Toward War

27. Jacob Siegel, "ISIS Is Using Social Media to Reach You, Its New Audience," Daily Beast, August 31, 2014. www.thedaily beast.com.
28. Quoted in Jethro Mullen, "Why Is ISIS Taunting the West?," CNN, September 22, 2014. www.cnn.com.
29. Quoted in Marc A. Thiessen, "Defense Intelligence Agency Warned Obama About ISIS in 2012," American Enterprise Institute, November 20, 2015. www.aei.org.
30. Quoted in Warrick, *Black Flags*, p. 279.
31. Hillary Rodham Clinton, *Hard Choices*. New York: Simon & Schuster, 2014, p. 392.
32. Quoted in NBC News, "Britain's David Cameron on ISIS: 'These People Want to Kill Us,'" September 23, 2014. www .nbcnews.com.

33. Quoted in Rebecca Kaplan, "Obama Will Strike ISIS 'Wherever They Exist,' Including Syria," CBS News, September 10, 2014. www.cbsnews.com.

34. Quoted in Peter Beinart, "How Serious a Threat Is ISIS?," *Atlantic*, September 11, 2014. www.theatlantic.com.

35. Quoted in Kaplan, "Obama Will Strike ISIS 'Wherever They Exist,' Including Syria."

36. Quoted in Spencer Ackerman and Raya Jalabi, "US Military Considers Sending Combat Troops to Battle Isis Forces in Iraq," *Guardian* (Manchester, UK), November 13, 2014. www.theguardian.com.

37. Quoted in Mark Landler and Jeremy W. Peters, "US General Open to Ground Forces in Fight Against ISIS in Iraq," *New York Times*, September 16, 2014. www.nytimes.com.

Chapter Four: Laying Siege to the Caliphate

38. Quoted in Rukmini Callimachiaug, "Inside Syria: Kurds Roll Back ISIS, but Alliances Are Strained," *New York Times*, August 10, 2015. www.nytimes.com.

39. Quoted in Callimachiaug, "Inside Syria."

40. Quoted in Callimachiaug, "Inside Syria."

41. Quoted in Robin Wright, "A Victory in Kobani?," *New Yorker*, January 27, 2015. www.newyorker.com.

42. Quoted in Helene Cooper and Eric Schmitt, "US Commandos Kill an ISIS Leader in Syria," *New York Times*, May 17, 2015, p. A1.

43. Quoted in Jim Michaels, "US Coalition Slashes ISIS Oil Revenue by More than 90 Percent," *USA Today*, October 2, 2017. www.usatoday.com.

44. Quoted in Gordon Corera, "IS Conflict: How Is It Getting Hold of Weapons from the West?," BBC News, November 21, 2016. www.bbc.com.

45. Ivor Prockett, "On Mosul's Front Line: A Grueling Battle on Civilian Streets," *New York Times*, June 5, 2017. www.nytimes.com.

46. Quoted in Qassim Abdul-Zahra and Susannah George, "Iraq Says Islamic State Is Defeated," *Philadelphia Inquirer*, December 10, 2017, p. A6.

Chapter Five: The War Continues

47. Quoted in Tom Winter, Jonathan Dienst, and Tracy Connor, "Attempted Terrorist Attack: Suspect Held After NYC Rush-Hour Blast," *NBC News*, December 11, 2017. www.nbc news.com.

48. Quoted in Winter, Dienst, and Connor, "Attempted Terrorist Attack."

49. Quoted in Benjamin Hart, "NYC Subway Bombing Suspect Wrote Anti-Trump Facebook Post Before Attack," *New York Magazine*, December 12, 2017. http://nymag.com.

50. Quoted in Katie Worth, "Lone Wolf Attacks Are Becoming More Common—and More Deadly," *Frontline*, PBS, July 14, 2016. www.pbs.org.

51. Quoted in Kate Irby, "FBI Cites Homegrown Terrorists," *Philadelphia Inquirer*, December 26, 2017, p. A6.

52. Quoted in NBC News, "Thanksgiving Day Parade Security Tight in Terror-Wary New York City," November 22, 2017. www.nbcnews.com.

53. Quoted in Laurel Wamsley, "Hawaii Mounts Legal Challenge to President's Revised Travel Ban," NPR, March 8, 2017. www.npr.org.

54. Quoted in Robin Wright, "ISIS Jihadis Have Returned Home by the Thousands," *New Yorker*, October 23, 2017. www .newyorker.com.

55. Quoted in Tom Rogan, "ISIS Is Still a Threat, Especially to the UK," *Washington Examiner*, December 28, 2017. www. washingtonexaminer.com.

56. Benjamin Bahney and Patrick B. Johnston, "ISIS Could Rise Again," *Foreign Affairs*, December 15, 2017. www.foreign affairs.com.

FOR FURTHER RESEARCH

Books

Andrew J. Bacevich, *America's War for the Greater Middle East: A Military History*. New York: Random House, 2017.

Fawaz A. Gerges, *A History of ISIS*. Princeton, NJ: Princeton University Press, 2017.

Mark L. Haas and David W. Lesch, eds., *The Arab Spring: The Hope and Reality of the Uprisings*. Boulder, CO: Westview, 2016.

Azeem Ibrahim, *Radical Origins: Why We Are Losing the Battle Against Islamic Extremism—and How to Turn the Tide*. New York: Pegasus, 2017.

Joby Warrick, *Black Flags: The Rise of ISIS*. New York: Anchor, 2016.

Internet Sources

Chris Dalby, "Who Is Buying the Islamic State's Illegal Oil?," Oil price.com, September 30, 2014. https://oilprice.com/Energy /Crude-Oil/Who-Is-Buying-The-Islamic-States-Illegal-Oil.html.

Economist, "Islam and Slavery: The Persistence of History," August 22, 2015. www.economist.com/news/international/216 61812-islamic-states-revival-slavery-extreme-though-it-finds -disquieting-echoes-across.

Fazel Hawramy, Shalaw Mohammed, and Kareem Shaheen, "Life Under Isis in Raqqa and Mosul: 'We're Living in a Giant Prison,'" *Guardian* (Manchester, UK), December 9, 2015. www.theguard ian.com/world/2015/dec/09/life-under-isis-raqqa-mosul-giant -prison-syria-iraq.

Jacob Siegel, "ISIS Is Using Social Media to Reach You, Its New Audience," Daily Beast, August 31, 2014. www.thedailybeast .com/isis-is-using-social-media-to-reach-you-its-new-audience.

Derek Stoffel, "Life Under ISIS: Mosul Residents Reflect on a Brutal Occupation," CBC News, March 22, 2017. www.cbc.ca

/news/world/life-under-isis-mosul-residents-reflect-on-a-brutal-occupation-1.4034574.

Ben Taub, "Journey to Jihad: Why Are Teen-agers Joining ISIS?," *New Yorker*, June 1, 2015. www.newyorker.com/magazine/2015/06/01/journey-to-jihad.

Katie Worth, "Lone Wolf Attacks Are Becoming More Common—and More Deadly," *Frontline*, PBS, July 14, 2016. www.pbs.org/wgbh/frontline/article/lone-wolf-attacks-are-becoming-more-common-and-more-deadly.

Robin Wright, "ISIS Jihadis Have Returned Home by the Thousands," *New Yorker*, October 23, 2017. www.newyorker.com/news/news-desk/isis-jihadis-have-returned-home-by-the-thousands.

Websites

Central Intelligence Agency (www.cia.gov). Through its *World Factbook*, the US government's chief spy agency provides background information on the dangers posed to visitors to numerous countries. Interested persons can find updates on the tenuous situations in Iraq and Syria, including maps, the state of their governments, and the terrorism threats they face.

Federal Bureau of Investigation (www.fbi.gov). The federal government's chief law enforcement agency maintains a web page that explains how it investigates terrorism on US soil. By following the link for Nationwide Suspicious Activity Reporting (NSAR), visitors can learn how local police departments are being trained by the FBI to recognize suspicious activity that could lead to acts of terrorism.

Global Coalition to Defeat ISIS (www.state.gov/s/seci). Established by the US State Department, this site explains the goals and accomplishments of the Global Coalition. By following the link for Travel Advisories, visitors can find country-by-country terrorism threats and learn what precautions should be taken when traveling overseas.

Kurdish Project (https://thekurdishproject.org). Established by Kurdish American entrepreneur Farhad Khosravi, the Kurdish Project seeks to explain the plight of the Kurdish people, their desire for a homeland, and their role in the war against ISIS. By following the website's link for Op-Ed, visitors can read the essay "The Kurds' Heroic Stand Against ISIS."

Operation Inherent Resolve (www.inherentresolve.mil). This website is maintained by the US Central Command, which coordinates the efforts of the US Army, Navy, Air Force, and Marines in the war against ISIS. The website includes news updates on the military's activities to combat ISIS.

Religion Library: Sunni Islam (www.patheos.com/library/sunni -islam). Hosted by Patheos.com, an Internet-based resource on world religions, this website explains the tenets of Sunni Islam. The site contains many resources on the founding, influences, and development of Sunni Islam and the circumstances that led to the break with the followers of Shia Islam.

United Nations Office of Counter-Terrorism (www.un.org/en /counterterrorism). Maintained by the United Nations, this website reports on activities of the Office of Counter-Terrorism set up by the UN to coordinate international efforts to respond to ISIS, al Qaeda, and other terrorist organizations. By following the link for Key Documents, visitors can read a 2017 report assessing the danger ISIS continues to pose to world peace.

Yazda (www.yazda.org). Yazda advocates for the rights of the Yazidis—the religious sect whose members have been murdered and enslaved by ISIS. Visitors can read about the work of attorney Amal Clooney—the wife of film star George Clooney—who helped persuade the United Nations to investigate war crimes by ISIS against the Yazidis.

INDEX

PICTURE CREDITS

Cover: iStockphoto.com

4: Georgios Kollidas/Shutterstock.com (top left); Dan Howell/Shutterstock.com (bottom left); iStockphotos.com (bottom right)

5: EnginKorkmaz (top); Orlok/Shutterstock.com (bottom)

8: Dabiq/ZUMA Press/Newscom

11: Associated Press

14: CEERWAN AZIZ/Reuters/Newscom

18: SalamPix/ABACA/Newscom

23: Bas Bogaerts/Polaris/Newscom

28: Kyodo

31: Lukasz Z/Shutterstock.com

34: Associated Press

38: Associated Press

42: State Department/Public Domain

47: Associated Press

50: STRINGER/Reuters/Newscom

54: Maury Aaseng

58: maphotostwo739344

62: Associated Press

66: Associated Press

ABOUT THE AUTHOR

Hal Marcovitz is a former newspaper reporter and columnist. He has written nearly two hundred books for young readers. Marcovitz makes his home in Chalfont, Pennsylvania.